When Life
Throws You a Curve

When Life Throws You a Curve

Divine Strategies for Handling
Whatever Life Throws at You

BY BILLY JOE DAUGHERTY

Destiny Image® Publishers, Inc.
P.O. Box 310
Shippensburg, PA 17257-0310

"Speaking to the Purposes of God for This Generation
and for the Generations to Come"

For Worldwide Distribution, Printed in the U.S.A.

ISBN 10: 0-7684-2363-5

ISBN 13: 978-0-7684-2363-1

Previously published as 1-5778-061-2 by Albury Publishing, Tulsa, OK

1 2 3 4 5 6 7 8 9 10 11 / 09 08 07 06

This book and all other Destiny Image, Revival Press, MercyPlace, Fresh Bread, Destiny Image Fiction, and Treasure House books are available at Christian bookstores and distributors worldwide.

For a U.S. bookstore nearest you, call
1-800-722-6774.

For more information on foreign distributors, call
717-532-3040.

Or reach us on the Internet:
www.destinyimage.com

Contents

Foreword

WHAT A GREAT PLEASURE it is to write this foreword to Pastor Billy Joe's new book—and I especially like the title, *When Life Throws You a Curve*. As a full-time minister, I have had some *monumental* curve balls thrown at me! But I also know that whether you're in the ministry from a pulpit or in a factory, a corporation, or a classroom, you will face some curve balls. That's another reason I love this book: It's for everyone.

Pastor Billy Joe is one of the Church's experts on dealing with curve balls. I can say that because through the years I have seen Pastor Billy Joe and his wife, Sharon, face and handle one curve ball after another. One reason their ministry and church have flourished is because they have learned how to deal with all the types of adversity the enemy has thrown at them. Some of those experiences are related in this book.

The knowledge and wisdom we can glean from this book is invaluable. Pastor Billy Joe not only gives solid truth from God's Word to stand on in times of crisis and difficulty, but he shows us clearly *how* to do it. His analogies to the game of baseball bring new light to truths we have known but have been unable to integrate into our lives.

Believe me, if you ever have been totally undone because something unexpected and unwanted came into your life, *When Life Throws You a Curve* is just what you need!

—Joyce Meyer
New York Times bestselling author
and renowned Bible teacher

Introduction

Curve Balls Are a Part of Life

MOST KIDS growing up in America—male and female—spend at least some time playing baseball or softball. Even if they do not play in a formal league, they usually play in their yard with plastic bats and balls.

As I was thinking about writing this book, I thought about my own years growing up playing Little League and then American Legion Baseball. One of the most challenging things was learning how to hit a curve ball when I was just a young teenager.

I remember how I could hit the straight pitches easily, and in Little League, that was all pitchers were allowed to throw. They would not let the Little League pitchers throw curve balls. When the pitch came—we called it a fast ball—it came straight across the plate and it was very easy to hit.

However, when I got a little older, the pitchers were allowed to throw curve balls. Have you ever tried to hit a curve ball? Well, even if you do not know (or particularly care) what a curve ball is, there is a good lesson for every person in this example!

A curve ball starts going one way and then goes another. A well-thrown fast ball is predictable—you know where it is going—and because of that, it is fairly easy to hit. But a curve ball is different. The pitcher makes the ball curve by pulling down on it with his fingers as he releases it. The ball spins diagonally and then curves.

I bat right-handed, so if a left-handed pitcher throws a curve to me, the ball curves toward me. If a right-hander is pitching to me, the ball curves away from me. Now that may sound like a relatively simple concept—something you just realize and adjust to—but it makes a big difference in your batting. In fact, lack of success at hitting curve balls is a major reason why a lot of kids quit playing baseball after Little League.

The fast ball and the curve ball *look* the same when the pitcher first releases the ball. So batters have to train their senses not to be moved by what they see. In other words, they cannot trust the path the ball *appears* to be on when the pitcher first releases it. Instead, they have to learn to watch the way the pitcher holds his wrist—because that is the key to knowing if the ball will be a fast ball, a curve, a slider, or whatever.

Then the batter has to adjust the timing of his swing to anticipate the ball's position when it reaches the plate. It is not an easy thing to do, even for the professionals, and even the greatest hitters strike out sometimes.

It is just like life. There are many times when people are not correctly handling problems and obstacles in their lives because they have failed to make an adjustment in their timing. They get ahead of God in some situation because they are treating it the same way they treated the previous situation. The point is this: Most of us are accustomed to handling things straight on, so it can be very difficult when we get a curve ball thrown at us.

When I say a curve ball, I am referring to an unexpected problem, a surprise obstacle, or a twist in the way you thought things were going to happen. For example, you thought your marriage was going to be everything you hoped for and you were going to live happily ever after. Then you found yourself in what seemed like a hornet's nest with the man or woman you married. There were personality conflicts, problems with your children or relatives, or maybe there were financial difficulties.

Maybe you were hired for a new job and you thought it was going to go a certain way, but then you found out that you had a boss or an employee who was a real pain in the neck. That was a curve ball. You did not see it coming. It started out the way you thought it would, but suddenly there was a change.

Perhaps you moved to a new city, thinking certain things were going to happen. But you got there and everything that was planned ended up changing. The opportunity you were so sure was there disappeared. What do you do in situations like these? That's what this book is all about!

When you have a situation with unexpected circumstances, you go to the rock: the Word of the living God. Jesus said that in this world we were going to experience tribulation and difficulties, but He told us that in Him we could have peace. And He also told us we could be of good cheer. You can have joy in a world where there is tribulation, because if you are in Him, then you have already overcome the world. (See John 16:33.) Christ has overcome the things that are trying to overcome you. Therefore if Christ is in you, that makes you an overcomer of whatever is trying to overcome you.

Another way to look at it is this: In the ocean there are sharks, but in the boat there is safety. You can stay in the boat (Jesus) and cross the ocean (go through life in this world), and the sharks will not get to you. In Christ there is victory, joy, and peace. In the world, there is tribulation, but in Christ, you can go through the world overcoming every circumstance and situation. It does not change the things that are in the world; it just changes your ability to overcome the world.

This book may not prevent you from experiencing some of the curve balls in life, but if you will give close attention to the principles given for handling them, you can be a record-breaking, major league hitter in your spiritual life!

Chapter 1

THE APOSTLE PAUL was a man who went through a lot of tribulation and faced many curve balls in life. He wrote about half the books in the New Testament, and those books are filled with God's wisdom about how we are supposed to face the difficulties that come into our own lives.

One of those situations is described in Acts 27. On his way to Rome, Paul's ship was almost lost in a fierce storm in the Mediterranean Sea. Previously, in Acts 21, he had been arrested in Jerusalem because of his preaching. The religious leaders of the day had opposed him, and it caused a riot. He was taken into custody, and when he stood for the hearing, he said, "I appeal to Caesar." Being a Roman citizen, Paul had that right. So they said, "Okay, you go to Rome and you will stand trial before Caesar." God had revealed to Paul that he was going to go to Rome to preach.

They left Caesarea by sea, heading out into the Mediterranean. At first, their journey kept them fairly close to the land as they sailed north around Cyprus, west along the coast of Galatia, and then to the island of Crete. As they changed ships, God spoke to Paul that if they launched at that time, they would encounter a terrific storm. There would be destruction of the ship and probably loss of life.

Paul went to the captain of the ship and said, "Do not sail." But the captain, instead of listening to Paul, listened to his crew and his own thinking, and they set sail. The storm hit just as they were away from the port, and they were driven by the wind until it looked as if they would all drown. In that moment, God spoke to Paul. He gave him a revelation of what would happen to him and why he must get to Rome.

Let us back up in this story and look at Acts 27. Sometimes circumstances look really good, as if the pitch will go straight across the plate, but looks can be deceiving, and a curve ball is really headed your way. The ship's captain sailed because it looked good, rejecting Paul's revelation and counsel.

> When a gentle south wind began to blow, they thought they had obtained what they wanted; so they weighed anchor and sailed along the shore of Crete. Before very long, a wind of hurricane force, called the "northeaster," swept down from the island. The ship was caught by the storm and could not head into the wind; so we gave way to it and were driven along. As we passed to the lee of a small island called Cauda, we were hardly able to make the lifeboat secure. When the men had hoisted it aboard, they passed ropes under the ship itself to hold it together.
>
> Fearing that they would run aground on the sand-bars of Syrtis, they lowered the sea anchor and let the ship be driven along. We took such a violent battering from the storm that the next day they began to throw the cargo overboard. On the third day, they threw the ship's tackle overboard with their own hands.
>
> (Acts 27:13-19 NIV)

The ship Paul was sailing on was an Alexandrian grain freighter, its cargo bound for sale in Italy. But two days into the storm, they tossed the cargo overboard to keep from running aground on quicksand. The third day, still trying to lighten the weight of the ship, they threw the ropes and the riggings overboard. The ropes and riggings that lift the ship's sails are now lying at the bottom of the sea. The curve balls are coming thick and fast. Let us continue in Acts 27:20:

> *When neither sun nor stars appeared for many days and the storm continued raging, we finally gave up all hope of being saved.*

This was not like an Oklahoma thunderstorm that blows up and passes through in an hour. Paul's ship was caught and held by what we would call a hurricane-type storm, literally being moved from north to south. There was no sailing out of it, and the sails could not be lifted even if they still had the tackle. They were trapped in a nightmare of wind and water. Day after day went by. There was no sun or stars because they were in the middle of the storm.

THE STORMS OF LIFE

This is a picture of what is happening right now in the earth. Storms have broken upon the nations. Storms have hit families and torn marriages apart. How many children today are crying because they do not know where their daddy is? Sometimes they do not even know who their daddy is. They do not know where Mommy is. Or perhaps the last they remember of Dad was seeing him get into his pickup truck and saying good-bye.

How many husbands and wives are suffering right now from the brokenness of divorce because a storm hit their home and their hearts have been ripped apart? How many people have an alcoholic or drug addict living in their home? Alcoholism and drug addiction are not things that pass after a week or two. This is a storm that rages year after year, beating on the lives of everyone in that home. What about someone who has an addiction to pornography, or someone who gambles the family into bankruptcy?

How many little children have been abused since they were three and four years old? Physically? Verbally? Sexually? Day in and day out, they are living in the middle of that storm—no peace, no hope; trapped and carried along by the circumstances.

How many are facing a diagnosis of a disease in their body for which there is no cure? Maybe it is a diagnosis of a mental disorder and the doctors say there is no hope. Maybe there was an accident that put the father or mother out of work for months. The medical bills are overwhelming, and they may lose their home because they cannot pay their bills.

We are not talking about just dozens of people. We are not talking about hundreds, and we are not talking about thousands. We are talking about millions and millions of people in our nation and around the world who are in the middle of such storms.

Vicious storms have hit our society, and the storms are intensifying. They are increasing. It is an hour like no hour in history. It is like a hurricane. Those huge storms build over the open water of the ocean, their winds often topping 100 miles per hour. When they make landfall in populated areas, the destruction is enormous. To make matters worse, it is not uncommon for tornadoes to be spawned when the hurricane comes inland. A tornado is a much smaller weather phenomenon, sometimes lasting only a few minutes, but its destructive power during its short life can be very great.

This is the big, slow-moving storm we are facing in America today: prayerless public schools, legalized abortion, rising divorce rates, alcoholism, drugs, and gangs. And the tornadoes spin off with deadly results: drive-by shootings, car wrecks caused by drunk drivers, and broken bones and broken hearts caused by domestic violence.

These are very difficult, stressful, oppressive times in which we are living. For many people, the description of their lives is found in this passage in Acts 27. They've given up all hope that they can be saved. Too many people have no hope that their family could ever be what they would call "normal." They do not even know what normal is, because they have never experienced it!

We have to understand what is going on in our society if we are going to have the heart that God wants us to have in this hour. Many people have their heads in the sand, some out of ignorance and others out of fear. Right now, we are going to lift our heads up, so that we can see and understand how to face the trials and the curve balls with the same spirit in which Paul faced them.

CAN ANYONE AVOID STORMS?

Storms hit all kinds of people: rich, poor, educated, uneducated, every race, and every neighborhood. Paul was a highly educated man, probably from an affluent Jewish family. He wrote much of the New Testament by God's inspiration, and yet in Acts 27 he was in the middle of one of many storms that hit his life.

> God has a plan
> to take us all the way to our destiny.

Some storms happen because of our own faults, failures, and mistakes. Sometimes we are where we shouldn't be, doing what we shouldn't be doing. But Paul did not make a mistake. He did not fail. He did not sin. In fact, he said, "There is going to be a storm. Do not sail." He saw the trouble, and he was trying to avoid it for himself and for the others. So what was the deal here?

Some storms happen because of the sins, failures, and mistakes of *other people*—people who have a direct impact on our lives—and that is just what happened in the case of Paul in Acts 27. Sometimes it is just circumstances in the society or nation in which we live that send a storm (or curve ball) our way. But the good news is, God has a plan to take us all the way to our destiny.

I want to share some things that you can use in your own life and to help others. We are going to face storms, but we are not prophesying negatively. It was Jesus who said, "In the world you will have tribulation; but be of good cheer, I have overcome the world" (John 16:33). The word *tribulation* here means "tribulation!" In the original Greek that word means pressure, anguish, persecution, and trouble. (See James Strong, *Greek Dictionary of the New Testament*, #2347.)

Jesus did not sugar-coat it. He said, "That is the way it is in the world." He did not say, "You might have it" or "It is a possibility." But He also said we could overcome these storms and have peace and joy. It is not enough just to have peace—and be gloomy. Let us go through this life *rejoicing*, living on the joy side of life.

Paul did not sugar-coat things, either. He said, "But know this, that in the last days perilous times will come" (2 Tim. 3:1). Paul said that the world system, a system that is against God, would also pressure us to fail and quit and even die. The lust of the flesh, the lust of the eyes, and the pride of life are a part of this world system. They are opposing the things of God. Therefore, if you are going for the kingdom of God, you are going to face those opposing forces. That is where the storm comes in!

WHAT TO DO?

What did Paul do in the face of this life-threatening storm in Acts 27?

But after long abstinence from food, then Paul stood in the midst of them and said, "Men, you should have listened to me, and not have sailed from Crete and incurred this disaster and loss. And now I urge you to take heart, for there will be no loss of life among you, but only of the ship. For there stood by me this night an angel of the God to whom I belong and whom I serve, Saying, 'Do not be afraid, Paul; you must be brought before Caesar; and indeed God has granted you all those who sail with you.' Therefore take heart, men, for I believe God that it will be just as it was told me."

(Acts 27:21-25)

Now that is a report to shout about! God is in control because Paul *gave* Him the control. They had 14 days of constant turmoil. That was two weeks with little sleep and little to eat. Fatigue, fear, and a ship full of men without hope. The game went into extra innings and weariness set in. There was no sun, no stars, just relentless wind and waves. But Paul never lost his connection with the Father. What was his strategy?

Number one, **Paul fasted.** Some of you are facing storms, and fasting a meal or two (a day or two) could help you get your spirit in tune with God. Fasting and prayer are found throughout the Bible, Old and New Testaments, as a pattern for people facing crises and difficult circumstances. When you fast and pray, your spirit gets stronger, more alert, and more energized. It is easier to bring your body and your mind under control.

When an overwhelming circumstance hits people and their spirit is not strong—they are not full of the Word and the Spirit of God—their mind will shift into panic and fear will grip their hearts. Some people actually go berserk. Others go into a state of shock and withdraw from everything and everyone, becoming recluses.

In many people today, with the devastating storms that have hit them, you can look into their eyes and see they have already "checked out." They may be typing at a typewriter or operating machinery in a plant somewhere, but you can see in their eyes and in the expression on their faces—or lack of expression—that there is "nobody at home." They are going through the motions of their job, they mow the lawn, drive to work, and cook their meals, but they are literally in a state of emotional shock because of the devastating curve balls and storms that have ravaged their lives.

When you and I take time to fast, our spirit—the part of us that contacts God—can begin to rise up. If you will feed your spirit (and maybe starve a little bit of that television time and other things that feed the mind and the emotional realm on worldly things), there will be a clarity of understanding so that you can interpret what God is saying to you. Then you can know what He is directing you to do.

Fasting and prayer are about bringing your body under control so that you tune out the demands of the flesh and tune in to God's instruction and guidance. Many times God is speaking, but people are so caught up in their emotions and the feelings of their body that they cannot interpret clearly what God is saying to them. Paul fasted and prayed, and when God spoke, he could clearly interpret what the Lord was saying. He could hear God inside his spirit, despite the roar of the storm.

*The second thing Paul did was that he **got into the presence of the Lord***. When we praise and worship, when we pray, when we read or listen to the Word of God, when we take time to acknowledge the Lord and get into His presence, we will be able to receive what God has for us.

Paul got into the presence of the Lord and *heard* from God. You have got to hear from Heaven. For Paul, it was through an angel. For you, it may be through prayer, God's Word, through a message preached from the pulpit, through a tape, or through reading a Christian book or magazine. The issue is that we must have a word from the Lord to hit that curve ball. It's God's Word that gives us peace and faith to overcome the circumstances that are coming at us.

In John 16:33, Jesus said, "These things have I *spoken* to you, that in Me you may have peace." If you do not hear Jesus speaking to you, you are not going to have peace. Even though He has spoken a lot of things and they are recorded in the Bible, you still need to hear it inside of your being and then receive it— that is the critical thing. Paul said, "For I believe God that it will be just as it was told me" (Acts 27:25).

Paul decided to believe God in the face of that storm. Many people say, "I will believe it when I see it, when I feel it, or when the conditions get better." But those who wait till then will probably never see the miracles of God. You have to choose to believe right in the middle of the storm and declare with your mouth, "I believe God." Say it out loud: "I believe God. It will be just like God said. What He said concerning my life shall come to pass!"

A third thing Paul did was that he **refused to be bitter and chose to be an encouragement instead** —*and the greatest encouragement is bringing people to God.* Even though he reminded the men that they shouldn't have launched out, he began to encourage them. He told them what the angel said to him. He told them they were not going to die (see Acts 27:22).

You know, Paul did not have to tell them about that angelic messenger. He could have come up on that deck and looked at those men and just thought to himself, "I am going to be saved. So what if all these thugs drown? It would serve them right for not listening to me when I told them this was going to happen."

You see, this was not the choir traveling with Paul. These were criminals, soldiers, and sailors. What do you think it sounded like on the deck of that ship when that storm hit? They were not singing, "This is the day that the Lord has made." They were not humming, "It is well with my soul." Have you been around any soldiers lately? Sailors? Or criminals? This was not the Sunday school picnic with Paul—and yet he encouraged them. Why? God said, "I have given you all those who sail with you."

I want to crack open your mind a little, lift up your head some, and get you to see this: *God has given you all those who are sailing with you.* Who is sailing with you? The people in your neighborhood, the people you contact as you walk through life. They are your relatives, your friends, and your business associates. You say, "But a bunch of them are not even saved. They do not even know God. Many of them are heathens." That was the crowd that was traveling with Paul!

> ## God has given you all those who are sailing with you.

Paul did not invite these guys to go with him on this missionary journey to Rome. No, he was dragged there in chains and locked up with them. These were people he did not know or have any association with. He was submitted to the rulership of these soldiers, who were ready to kill all the prisoners during the storm. They figured, "They are all going to drown, so let us kill them anyway—just have a little fun." That was the type of group Paul was sailing with—and he was encouraging them!

Right now, all over America, there are millions of Christians who have a revelation that they are going to make it to Heaven. God is with them. There is even a bunch who have a revelation that they are overcomers—that they have victory, joy, and peace in their lives. And you know what? They are sitting on the sidelines smugly saying, "I am glad I am not like this other bunch." They are looking down their noses at the people around them who are "prisoners, sailors, and soldiers," enslaved to this world's system.

We've got a lot of believers thinking how glad they are that they are not caught up in alcoholism or drugs. They are glad their children are not being abused. They are happy that all of their bills are paid and that they are not facing financial bankruptcy. They are thinking about all the bad things they see on television, what is happening in difficult parts of the world, and they are thinking, "Oh, I am glad I am not like that, and that is not happening to me."

We must wake up! The Lord is knocking on our doors today and saying, "I did not save you just so you could get to Heaven. I want you to take all those who are sailing with you—all those people you come in contact with in your life. You know, the ones you did not necessarily ask for, that you did not invite into a relationship, but God brought them across your life for a divine purpose. God determined that He would bring them into contact with you because He knew you would listen to Him. And if you would listen to Him, then you could tell them about Me."

You need to determine right now, in the midst of your storm, "I am going to reach out and compel people to come into the Kingdom of God. I am not going to let anybody jump ship." Those soldiers and several of the criminals tried to do just that, and Paul could have looked at them and said, "Well, all those guys are going to drown. If they had only obeyed what I said, they could have been saved." But do you know what Paul did? Look at Acts 27:31:

> Paul said to the centurion and the soldiers, "Unless these men stay in the ship, you cannot be saved." Then the soldiers cut away the ropes of the skiff and let it fall off.

In other words, some of them were going to try to escape in the little boat they'd pulled on board earlier. Today, we would call it a lifeboat. And that was exactly what some of the men on board thought it was going to be for them. But like people all around us, they were deceived, so Paul went after them. He compelled them to stay in the ship, to trust God's Word.

Jesus told the story in Luke 14 of a great banquet that was planned. All the preparations had been made and the master of the banquet sent out his servants to invite all the people to come to the table. One by one, as the servants went out to invite people, the people began to make excuses. One said, "I just bought a new set of oxen. I have to go test them." Another said, "I bought some land. I have to go look over it." Another said, "I have just gotten married and I have to take care of my family." Business, real estate, and family. Things to do, places to go, people to see. They had no time for the Kingdom of God.

When the servants returned and the master heard those words, the Bible says he was angry. It is a picture of our heavenly Father. Those who were invited refused to come, and the master said:

> Go out quickly into the streets and lanes of the city, and bring in here the poor and the maimed and the lame and the blind. Go out into the highways and hedges, and compel them to come in, that my house may be filled.
>
> (Luke 14:21,23)

You see, when we are talking about bringing people to Christ, it is not some nice little invitation. Jesus said, "Compel them to come in." He's saying, "You persuade them; you fill My house." Paul said, "Those men have got to get back in the ship. We are not letting anybody jump off."

We have let too many people go to hell when the curve balls come and the storms hit because we are consumed with our own problems instead of God's Word. We miss the fact that because of that curve ball we are rubbing shoulders with people we normally wouldn't and they aren't saved. This is one way God takes the curve balls and turns them to His and our good. We bring people into the Kingdom!

We have let too many people jump ship and we have not gone after them. It is time we wake up and say, "We are not going to let people go to hell just because we are in the middle of a storm. We are not going to let them jump ship without our doing everything we can to let them know they have got to stay on board the ark of salvation. They have got to give their lives to Jesus."

Picture Paul in that boat. There was only one way to survive, and he knew what it was. He did not keep it to himself. He said, "You have got to stay in this boat." We know there is only one way too. There is only one way to gain eternal life and escape eternal damnation. His name is Jesus and He is the *only way*. (See John 14:6.)

What is going to cause us to be concerned about others? We should not just think, "Poor little ol' me. I am going through struggles. I am going through trials. I am overwhelmed. Oh, pray for me, brother. I need all the help I can get." That is a picture of a lot of Christians. They are faithful, dues-paying members of the "P.L.O.M. Club" (poor little ol' me club). Have you ever been there? Are you the only member on your block? Do not get me wrong; I have been in that same club myself! And then I realized I did not like that membership and I had to get out of it—to save myself and to save others.

The fourth thing Paul remembered during the storm was that **he had a destiny**. God had told him, "You are going to preach in Rome. I have called you for that." (See Acts 23:11.) Do you know what is going to help you get through your overwhelming circumstances? It is a revelation of your destiny. Be like Joseph of old. Even in those chains, rejected by his brothers in the pit, slandered by a woman who tried to seduce him, Joseph had a dream that he would not let go of. He lost a lot of coats, but he did not lose his dream!

In Acts 27, Paul was losing it all, but he did not lose his vision. David said, "I would have lost heart, unless I had believed that I would see the goodness of the Lord in the land of the living" (Ps. 27:13).

You may be in an overwhelming circumstance right now, but God is lifting up the light of His Word to let you know you have a future and a hope. He says, "I have plans for you, and they are plans for good and not for evil." (See Jeremiah 29:11.) When you get hold of that, you will rise up out of your despair. I am talking about resurrection! If you've been knocked down, buried, and the stone has been rolled in place, today Jesus is saying to you, "I've rolled away the stone, so come forth!"

Become compassionate for others and realize you have a destiny, a goal to be reached. Then press toward it in spite of the unexpected storms—or curve balls—that come your way, just as Paul did in Acts 27.

What happened when Paul refused to give up on these soldiers, criminals, and sailors? They were delivered from the jaws of death and so was he!

You and those who sail with you will also be delivered when the curve balls come if you will listen to God, trust and obey Him.

Chapter 2

How a Mother Dealt With a Curve

WHEN THAT CURVE BALL comes rushing at you and you hear from Heaven, then you have to decide, *I believe God*. That was the decision one of our members, Fannie Turentine, had to make when a terrible storm hit her life. Fannie's teenage son, Deondre, was shot to death by gang members as he rode his bicycle near their apartment home. Deondre was not involved with the gangs; he was just caught in the cross fire between rival gang members.

Now Fannie knew that God did not cause her son's death, that the devil was the author of his murder, but her grief was intense. Then, in the midst of her tragedy, Fannie heard God say, "All things work together for good to those who love God" (Rom. 8:28). In the sorrow and heartbreak of losing her child, Fannie heard the word of the Lord and decided to believe the Word of God.

God showed Fannie that she could make a difference in the lives of young people in the housing projects. She stood up before our congregation and testified that she was holding three different Bible studies in her home each week, one of them for elementary school boys that lived nearby.

From the world's point of view, Fannie had every reason to get bitter. She had every reason to hate. But she decided to believe God that out of her loss, God could bring gain. Out of what the devil intended for evil, God could bring good. Fannie saw that because she forgave, her other children could forgive too. Lives have been changed and people brought into the Kingdom of God because Fannie believed the Word of the Lord.

The day came when Fannie received a letter—a letter that was a remarkable testimony to God's promise. The letter was from one of the five young men convicted of Deondre's murder. This is what he wrote:

> To the mother of Deondre Turentine:
>
> Ma'am, even though I know how little words are as an offering, comfort, or compensation, I still send my apologies and regrets for the loss of your son. No man can ever feel the pain equivalent to a mother losing a child, but I assure you that I am no stranger to the loss of a loved one. I was convicted of murdering your son, but I was not his murderer. Please do not misunderstand my position. I do not deny responsibility or involvement in your son's death. I just did not have the murder weapon in my hands. That may sound like a cop-out to you, but it is the truth.
>
> It is also the truth that I have accepted full responsibility for your son's death. Taking the blame for Deondre's death has served to save my life by realizing the pain I caused, not only to you, but to my own mother and the mothers of my friends as well. By realizing the position that I put myself in, I have decided never to jeopardize myself or my loved ones again because of my stupidity or ignorance.
>
> My life was saved on the day that I was sentenced for my crime. I was on the verge of suicide and eternal death, then my preacher said, "Do not take your life. Give it to Christ." That day my life was saved, and it would still be lost if not for the loss of your son.

Knowing God now, I can offer you comfort in a few ways. First and foremost, your son's death—though foolish, it was not meaningless. Getting my life straight has been a monumental relief to my mother's spirit. My life has been dedicated to saving kids from Deondre's fate. Second, I believe your son's suffering has ended, and he is sitting with God in Heaven. That, Ma'am, is the greatest comfort offered to any man or woman on earth.

God gave Fannie the strength to share that letter with us, and then she said this:

Deondre and I had prayed for the teenagers that were involved in his life. One came by my house last Saturday night. I am using this letter to show them. This one young man—he cried so. You know, he just grabbed me, and he said, "Ma'am, please continue to keep me in your heart." He just dropped by to see how Deondre's Mom was doing. But I had to share this testimony with him, because they need to know, they really need to know that sin will destroy them, but God came that we might have life and have it more abundantly.

I know the young man who wrote this letter is in prison, but he has life, and he has it more abundantly. You know, that is the most important thing. It is not where you are, because I live in a low-income apartment. Maybe my desire is not to be there, but as Esther said, "For such a time as this," and I just thank God. I thank God for opening my heart to Him and that He has given me truth and revelation, truth that is even now setting me free. You know, there is a depth that you will never reach in Christ. He is so wide, you cannot go around Him. He is so deep, you cannot reach the bottom. He is so high...He is just all-powerful. He is right here, but yet He is in all 50 states and oh so many coun-tries. He is just omnipresent. He is God and He is real.

Why are children and teenagers coming to Fannie's house and getting saved? Why is it that a young man convicted of murder got saved in prison? It is because someone decided to believe God in the face of an adverse circumstance and horrible grief.

The day Fannie came down in front of the congregation and shared her testimony, I was preaching on overcoming difficult circumstances. Fannie pretty much preached my whole message with her life! We did not even discuss it beforehand; the Holy Ghost set it up. I could have preached a good sermon and made a lot of good points about believing God and refusing to get bitter, but Fannie lived it.

Fannie Turentine thought her son would grow up and be all God intended him to be, but satan turned that straight pitch into a terrible curve. Nevertheless, because Fannie heard God's Word, trusted Him and His Word, and acted on His Word, many lives have been saved. When she hit that curve ball with God's Word, He honored her faith with results that will last into eternity—and He will do the same for you, no matter what you're facing.

Chapter 3

When My Mother Faced a Curve

W E MAY GO THROUGH adverse circumstances, but we do not have to stop and keep company with them. When my father died in an accident many years ago, Mom immediately had to deal with it. It initially devastated her life. She was destroyed emotionally. My brother got the call first, and he called me in Tulsa from Kansas. He said he was on his way down to Arkansas and would pick us up on the way. My mother was sedated medically to bring her under control.

I said, "I have got to call her before we leave tonight." At that moment, my mother's house was filled with friends, neighbors, and people that we had known for years. I called and talked to the people there. "I have to talk to Mom," I said. So they literally lifted her up and brought her to the phone. I began to speak the Word of God to her.

Remember, Jesus said, "These things I have spoken to you, that in Me you may have peace" (John 16:33). When the Word of God comes, it can bring peace.

I told my mother that Jesus would never leave her, that He would strengthen her, and that He would help her. (See Psalm 46:1.) I said that He is the "lifter" (see Ps. 3:3) and that He was doing it right at that moment, and then we prayed. You know, the anointing breaks the yoke of bondage. People testified that when she hung up the phone, she was a changed woman. Why? The anointed Word of God changes everything.

You may be reading this and you are in a zombie-like state. Maybe your husband or wife walked off. Maybe you are going through the death of a loved one, or your finances are in shambles, or a report from the doctor has hit you like a ton of bricks and you are overwhelmed with it. This word is coming to you to wake you up, to bring you to attention. You are going to make it! You are going to overcome.

After the funeral, the Lord told me to speak a word to my mother. I said, "Mom, you can spend the rest of your life in a rocking chair, thinking about how it was and living in the memories of it, or you can rise up and begin to reach out to other people and give them the love and comfort and encouragement that *you* need. If you do that, you will be healed."

This was a key to hitting curve balls that I had learned at Oral Roberts University: Seed-faith. Seed-faith is simply planting a seed for what you need, and it is not just about money; it is about every area in your life. If you need money, give money; if you need friends, be a friend; if you need to hear from God, spend time in His Word and in prayer. If you need love, give your love to others.

Mom made a decision. In fact, that very next week after the memorial service, she started going to nursing homes— and she was not a minister. She was the secretary and traffic manager of a radio station. But she started going to the nursing homes after she got off work, and she would go into the rooms of people she did not even know. She began to put her arms around old women and old men who had been forgotten. Their kids had not visited them in years, but she began to love them. And instead of her life being overwhelmed, she became an overcomer. Now Mom is in her seventies, serving on our church staff with us and still loving people.

I do not know what you are going through, what curve ball is being hurled at you. But I do know that the power of God can help you get through it if you plant a seed for what you need right now.

Chapter 4

Sharon Hits Some Curve Balls

NOT TOO LONG AGO, my wife Sharon went through an overwhelming time in her life. We had just come back from Africa, where we were involved in a wonderful crusade. But we returned home to a packed week, starting with her ladies' seminar. Then we had to move the date we were scheduled to record a live worship tape to the Sunday evening service on the same weekend.

Now a live recording is not like recording in a studio, where you can record one song and go back to make changes or corrections if you need to. This was 45 minutes that had to be right the first time. And the pressure was not just to know all the songs, but each song had to have back-up vocals, musical accompaniment, and technical work.

Sharon leads our music ministry, so she was responsible for working with all of our people to coordinate the project and get everything lined up ahead of time. Now a "curve ball" in the scheduling threw the recording into the very same weekend she was holding the ladies' seminar.

Not only was Sharon ministering in the ladies' meetings, but she had special guest speakers coming in and also was handling all the details that go with a conference where hundreds of ladies are expected to attend. If that wasn't overwhelming enough, she felt a responsibility to her family.

But there was more! To top it off, it was the month of May. Next to Word Explosion week in the summer, May is the busiest time of year at Victory Christian Center. This is the month of all the graduation ceremonies and activities for Victory Christian School, Victory Bible Institute, and the World Missions Training Center. Then there are the normal responsibilities that go with Sunday and Wednesday services. So Sharon felt even more overwhelmed.

The good news is, we had a great recording and over 900 ladies attended the conference activities. But Sharon still came away with an overwhelmed feeling. Some people would call it frazzled! You may feel like you are there today. Have you ever— especially if you are a wife and mother—felt like you had so many things to do with the kids, the shopping, the house, and your job that you felt like one of those people you used to see on television years ago who would try to keep all the plates spinning on top of a bunch of poles? They would run frantically back and forth to keep the plates spinning, trying to catch any that fell to keep them from shattering on the floor.

> What you need most of all when you're faced with curve ball after curve ball is to get into God's presence.

Even after Sharon had the recording session and the conference behind her, there were still a lot of plates up there spinning and needing her attention. One of them was a worship seminar with a special guest music minister the following Thursday through Sunday. On the Friday night of the seminar, the church had one of our all-night praise and prayer services. We opened that meeting with the guest minister leading our congregation in three hours of praise and worship.

As Sharon got into the presence of the Lord by praising and worshiping God, the presence of the Holy Spirit, the anointing, destroyed all of that overwhelmed feeling. It was just like it says in Isaiah 10:27, "The yoke will be destroyed because of the anointing." Absolutely nothing changed on Sharon's schedule; all the things were still there. But everything changed in Sharon. Hallelujah! God gave her the victory, joy, and peace.

You may think you need a vacation or a schedule change. If you can go on a vacation or work a change in your schedule, that is all right. But a vacation can only last so long, and it may not bring the rest and relaxation you anticipated. You may change your schedule, but it can get unexpectedly changed by other people and circumstances beyond your control. So you need to know what to do no matter how things go.

What you need most of all when you're faced with curve ball after curve ball is to get into God's presence. What happens when you get in God's presence? The Word of God tells us:

> *He restores my soul.*
>
> (Psalm 23:3)

> *In Your presence is fullness of joy.*
>
> (Psalm 16:11)

> *But those who wait on the Lord shall renew their strength; they shall mount up with wings like eagles, they shall run and not be weary, they shall walk and not faint.*
>
> (Isaiah 40:31)

Hallelujah!

Sharon had several curve balls thrown at her all at once, but when she began to praise and worship God, she hit that home run of coming into His presence—and we all went home rejoicing!

If you're totally overwhelmed with your circumstances, begin to praise God right now. Put on a worship tape and get into His presence. I promise you that He will meet you there and restore your joy and peace and strength!

Chapter 5

Staying in the Game

WHEN A BATTER is standing at the plate, there is no rule in baseball that says the pitcher can only throw one curve ball per batter. When people (or circumstances) pitch someone a curve ball, followed by another, then followed by another, many people react like the Little Leaguers who strike out and say, "I quit. I am throwing in the towel. I give up."

There are times when every believer experiences those feelings, but I want to give you some things that are going to help you. You see, the apostle Paul had some major curve balls thrown at him—some things he did not expect or plan. One of them happened right on the heels of that shipwreck.

The ship crashed and broke apart, but just as God had told Paul through the angel, all the men survived and made it to the island of Malta. Then, as he was gathering firewood, Paul was bitten by a snake—a deadly viper. Talk about a curve ball! He had just spent 14 days barely eating, riding out a terrible storm, and finally making it to shore with the others on broken pieces of the ship. He was just trying to help build a fire so they could get warm and dry out. He was not out there hunting poisonous snakes!

In Acts 28:5 it says, "He shook off the creature into the fire and suffered no harm." And when Paul did not fall down dead, the natives of the island were amazed. They told him that the chief of the island was sick and asked Paul to pray for him. When Paul prayed, the man was healed by the power of God. Then all the people on the island with diseases came to Paul and they were healed too.

What happened? In our language today, Paul might have said, "All right, devil, if you are going to throw curves, then set 'em up. I am gonna knock 'em out of the park. I did not plan on getting shipwrecked and snake bit, but if I am going to be here, I will get everybody on the island saved and healed."

Do you hear what I am saying? Sure you are experiencing some problems right now. You are faced with difficulties. We cannot deny it. I have thought about my own life as I have meditated on this word that I am sharing with you. I have probably had as many curve balls as I have had straight balls in my life. In other words, there are certain things you plan to happen in your life, on your job, with your family, and your kids. But there are times when things go "zingo." Suddenly something changes. You did not plan on it, but there it is, staring you in the face.

At those times, there are a lot of people who get mad at God and turn their anger on Him. Some identify people as their problem and get bitter toward them. Others get dismal, gloomy, and discontent. You'll hear them say, "You know, I never planned on this happening. All this junk has taken place and now my life's ruined." And then they check out—some by actually taking their own lives—many others by turning to drugs, alcohol, gambling, or wrong relationships.

It was not in the plan. We did not foresee this. We did not expect it. Curve balls come from many different sources. There are things that are thrown at us from the world, from the devil, and from our own flesh. But there are also times when God Himself will throw us a few curves. The good news is that He is going to give us a way to get base hits and home runs!

An illustration of what I'm talking about happened to Paul in Acts, chapter 16:

Now when they had gone through Phrygia and the region of Galatia, they were forbidden by the Holy Spirit to preach the word in Asia.

(Acts 16:6)

Now try to imagine that. There was Paul, a tireless preacher sent to the Gentiles by the God who says, "Go into all the world and preach the gospel to every creature" (Mark 16:15). Paul starts to go out and suddenly the Lord says, "Do not go to Asia." That was a curve ball!

*After they had come to Mysia, they tried to go into Bithynia, but **the Spirit did not permit them.***

(Acts 16:7)

Another curve ball! Paul must have been thinking, "Lord, I thought we were supposed to go and travel and preach the gospel." But God has stopped them twice. So they passed by Mysia and came down to Troas.

And a vision appeared to Paul in the night. A man of Macedonia stood and pleaded with him, saying, "Come over to Macedonia and help us." Now after he had seen the vision, immediately we sought to go to Macedonia, concluding that the Lord had called us to preach the gospel to them.

(Acts 16:9-10)

Paul must have thought, "Finally! This is the direction God wants us to take. We are going to go after it and see Him do great things!"

In Macedonia, the most important city was Philippi. In that city, there was a group of Jewish women who met along the river for prayer. Paul began to meet with them and explain that Jesus Christ, God's Son, had been sent for the forgiveness of their sins and God had raised Him from the dead. The leader of that little prayer group, Lydia, believed the gospel. Then more women began to believe, and a church started from that riverside prayer meeting.

For Paul, these were straight pitches. This was what he had been wanting to do and what he expected to happen. He was preaching the gospel and people were getting saved. Things were working like they were supposed to. After two curve balls, Paul finally was getting some straight balls.

But wait a minute—then came another curve.

> *Now it happened, as we went to prayer, that a certain slave girl possessed with a spirit of divination met us, who brought her masters much profit by fortune-telling.*
>
> (Acts 16:16)

A girl who was like a modern-day palm reader or fortuneteller, and who was owned by some men, began to follow Paul and the others with him.

In verse 17 it says the girl cried out, "These men are the servants of the Most High God, who proclaim to us the way of salvation." The only problem was, she was saying it to mock them and make fun of them. Now, that is a curve ball. Everybody else Paul has been talking to wants to hear the gospel, and revival was going on. But then came this harassment. Every day he went to preach and the girl was back there yelling at him.

> *And this she did for many days. But Paul, greatly annoyed, turned and said to the spirit, "I command you in the name of Jesus Christ to come out of her." And he came out that very hour.*
>
> (Acts 16:18)

In today's language he might have said, "I am going to knock this goofy curve ball out of here."

So the enemy fled. The demon came out and the girl was delivered. Paul hit the curve ball with a resounding smack.

Everybody was happy, right? The woman who was bound by a devil was set free. Paul did just what Jesus said we are to do—cast out devils. But there was another pitch bearing down on Paul—still another curve ball.

> But when her masters saw that their hope of profit was gone, they seized Paul and Silas and dragged them into the marketplace to the authorities.

> (Acts 16:19)

Paul had just been used by God for a great, wonderful miracle. A person being oppressed and bound by a demon was delivered and set free. Paul did the right thing, and for all his trouble he was grabbed illegally and roughly dragged before the governing officials of the city. His accusers said, "These men, being Jews, exceedingly trouble our city" (Acts 16:20). They were slandered for being Jews and then they were lied about. Paul and Silas were not making trouble; they were stopping trouble. A woman possessed by a demon was causing trouble, and God had used Paul to deliver her. Within minutes, what should have been a triumph got twisted into lies.

> They teach customs which are not lawful for us, being Romans, to receive or observe.

> (Acts 16:21)

Then the mob that had gathered rose up against Paul and Silas, and the magistrates tore off their clothes and commanded them to be beaten with rods. Now this was not the Roman scourge. This was rods. With the scourge they could only be whipped 39 times, but there was no limit to how many times they could be beaten with rods.

> And when they had laid many stripes on them, they threw them into prison, commanding the jailer to keep them securely. And having received such a charge, he

put them into the inner prison and fastened their feet in the stocks.

(Acts 16:23-24)

Paul must have been feeling like he was having one bad day at Black Rock—or in this case, Philippi. He and Silas were not taken to the outer minimum security area of the prison. They were thrown in the dungeon—maximum security and maximum misery—and their feet were locked into stocks.

Do you agree this was a major, big-time curve ball? Paul had obeyed God. He had gone where he was supposed to go. He came to Philippi. He was conducting Holy Spirit meetings. People were getting saved and set free. Everything was going right, but suddenly the bottom just dropped out. Now he was beaten and bloody, looking at the inside of a Philippian jail. Paul was probably thinking the same thoughts you or I would have been thinking. *What happened?*

A curve ball! Right now, you might be right in the middle of a marriage situation where a pitch has curved out on you. Maybe it is your finances, or maybe it is not just one curve ball, it is two or three or four. You had such high hopes, and things were looking so good at first, but over time things began to turn—one curve ball after another. Now you are tired, you are hurting, and you are ready to throw in the towel, give up, and quit. At this point, quitting looks good because you are too weary to care. What are you going to do?

Paul wrote his letter to the Romans a few years *after* his experience in Philippi. He talked about what had happened there. Think back to Romans 8:28. Paul said what? "All things work together for good."

Now these are the things you are going to have to get in your mind if you are going to hit a curve ball. You have to remember these principles when a curve ball comes at you so you will know how to respond. You may be facing so many things you did not plan on all at the same time, and you want to check out and not use your faith, not believe God's Word, not go after it, and not overcome. But the Lord is calling to you, "Get up to the plate! Stay in the game! *All things work together for good.* Believe it!"

Even though this may not have been what you planned on, start believing like Joseph, that all these things are going to work together for good because you love God and are called according to His purpose. Do you love the Lord with all your heart? Then hear this: God will work things together for good if you will love Him and walk according to His purpose. He has called you, He has justified you, and He has put Himself in you.

As you stand in front of the things you are battling, remember God is in you. He has put His call on your life, and He has declared you, "Not Guilty"! He has pardoned you, and if God is for you, who can be against you? Who can strike you out? *God is for you!*

You see, in the face of what you are going through, the devil is telling you, "Strike one, strike two, strike three, you are out of here." That is his plan for you. But God is the umpire, and He says, "Play ball!" You get to play until He helps you get a hit; until the two of you knock one out of the park together to the glory of Jesus Christ. "Shall He not with Him also freely give us all things?" (Rom. 8:32). God is going to give you whatever you need to hit curve ball after curve ball.

In baseball, you can knock a home run off a curve just as you can off a straight pitch. Once you learn how to time your swing, you can connect with it and send it soaring right out of the park. You may feel you can handle your life as long as everything goes just right. But you can also handle it if it goes all wrong! Paul asked if distress or persecution or famine or nakedness or peril could separate us from the love of God. Do those things change anything? *No!* In all these things, we are more than conquerors. (See Romans 8:37-39.)

It does not matter what pitch is thrown our way. Why? Because we are persuaded. "Neither life nor death, things that are present nor things to come, height, depth, principalities or powers, wicked spirits..." or *whatever* can separate us from God's love. Whatever pitch is thrown, we know that nothing is going to separate us from the love of God, which is in Christ Jesus.

What did Paul do as he bled and suffered in the Philippian jail? There at midnight, bleeding, in chains, in the inner prison, he and Silas began to do something.

> *But at midnight Paul and Silas were praying and singing hymns to God, and the prisoners were listening to them.*
>
> (Acts 16:25)

They were not singing softly, "Oh, bless the Lord (sigh). I hurt all over, but hallelujah anyway." No! They were inside the inner prison, but their voices were audible to all the prisoners in that jail. They were praising God with all their might! And what happened as a result?

> *Suddenly there was a great earthquake, so that the foundations of the prison were shaken; and immediately all the doors were opened and everyone's chains were loosed. And the keeper of the prison, awaking from sleep and seeing the prison doors open, supposing the prisoners had fled, drew his sword and was about to kill himself. But Paul called out with a loud voice, saying "Do yourself no harm, for we are all here." Then he called for a light, ran in, and fell down trembling before Paul and Silas. And he brought them out and said, "Sirs, what must I do to be saved?"*
>
> (Acts 16:26-30)

Oh, hallelujah! God can help you connect with that curve ball and hit a home run even if you're tired and beaten and ready to quit!

That night the jailer and all of his household got saved and baptized. The devil threw a curve, but Paul responded by starting a jailhouse revival. He knocked that curve clean out of the park! What happened in that jail launched the church at Philippi, to which Paul wrote:

> *Being confident of this very thing, that He who has begun a good work in you will complete it until the day of Jesus Christ.*
>
> (Philippians 1:6)

> *For it is God who works in you both to will and to do His good pleasure.*
>
> (Philippians 2:13)

> *Forgetting those things which are behind and reaching forward to those things which are ahead, I press toward the goal for the prize of the upward call of God in Christ Jesus.*
>
> (Philippians 3:13-14)

> *And my God shall supply all your need according to His riches in glory by Christ Jesus.*
>
> (Philippians 4:19)

> *Be anxious for nothing, but in everything by prayer and supplication, with thanksgiving, let your requests be made known to God.*
>
> (Philippians 4:6)

> *I know how to be abased, and I know how to abound. Everywhere and in all things I have learned both to be full and to be hungry, both to abound and*

to suffer need. I can do all things through Christ who strengthens me.

(Philippians 4:12-13)

In effect, Paul was saying, "It does not matter what pitch they throw—inside, outside, high, low, curve ball, principalities, powers, rulers of darkness—or how many come at me, I am staying in the game and God will help me hit 'em all."

Perhaps you are at a point in your life where you are thinking, "With all that has happened to me, it looks like it's over. It looks like I've lost. I'm whipped. I have made too big a mistake, so there is no way the promises of God will be fulfilled in my life." But as believers, we do not play nine-inning games! We play until we win!

> Today is your day to be delivered from the fear of not being able to handle the unexpected.

In baseball, if we strike out, we don't stop going to bat. We get right back up and expect to hit that home run. As Christians, if we sin, we repent, turn away from sin, and get even more focused on God and what He's called us to do. In other words, when the devil comes to us and says, "That's it. You're out. It's all over," we can respond, "No, I'm up to bat again. I'm going to play again. I will not quit, and I will hold steady until I win."

Do not call it over! Do not call it a game. Do not allow the devil to talk you into quitting and walking away from the fulfillment of the promises God has given you! You may think you are in a tomb. You may feel you have been buried and three days have gone by. But when it looked like it was all over for Jesus,

He knocked a home run on the third day! Jesus played until He won! He rose from the grave!

Today is your day to be delivered from the fear of not being able to handle the unexpected, of thinking you have failed because you did not know how to hit a curve ball, and of simply being worn out from hitting curve after curve.

Today is your day to rise up and squarely face those things you did not plan on. Even if you have been leveled by the devil, God is saying, "Get up to the plate. I am right here with you all the way. And we are going to play until we win!"

Chapter 6

Hold on to Your Bat!

GOD WILL SHOW YOU how to get base hits and home runs, but there is a part that God plays and a part that you play. And the part that you play often determines what part God will play.

In baseball, there is a time-honored tradition called spring training. To get in shape for the upcoming season, you must show up for training and work hard at it. Everyone on the team participates in spring training, from the rookies to the seasoned veterans. It is a time to improve their physical conditioning and *review the basics.*

If you are out of shape and your basic skills are rusty, even the best winning strategy will probably fall short. In other words, you are likely to strike out. If you have not been experiencing the kind of results you want in the Kingdom of God, maybe it is time for you to go back to spring training.

To "knock 'em out of the park," especially when curve balls come your way, the basics are simple: You need to know how to hold on to your bat. The same is true for spiritual spring training: You have to spend time in the Word and pray, and then speak it out in faith.

> *Grace and peace be multiplied to you in the knowledge of God and of Jesus our Lord, as His divine power has given to us all things that pertain to life and*

godliness, through the knowledge of Him who called us by glory and virtue, by which have been given to us exceedingly great and precious promises, that through these you may be partakers of the divine nature, having escaped the corruption that is in the world through lust.

(2 Peter 1:2-4)

God's promises are like seeds; and when they are mixed with faith, they will produce a crop of blessings in God's Kingdom. They will bring a harvest of the inheritance—Heaven on earth in your life.

God *desires* to give you all things pertaining to life and godliness—everything you need in the natural and spiritual realms. When you believe and receive the promises of God in your heart and mix faith with them, allowing His Word to work in you, you will begin to take on His character in addition to receiving His blessings and benefits. But you must *know* God's promises before you can obtain them.

> If you have not been experiencing the kind of results you want in the Kingdom of God, maybe it is time for you to go back to spring training.

This is how you hold onto your bat, by praying the promises of God's Word, which is His will. Then you will make a hit and receive the requests you have asked of Him. In First John 5:14-15, it says:

Now this is the confidence that we have in Him, that if we ask anything according to His will, He hears us.

And if we know that He hears us, whatever we ask, we know that we have the petitions that we have asked of Him.

> ## The profession of your faith is your confession of God's Word—in faith.

Once you understand God's promises are for you and you begin to pray in line with those promises, then you can be confident that He will answer you and perform His Word on your behalf.

You are not locking God in a box when you hold on to His Word. God's Word is His will. If you will learn the Word, you will learn how God sovereignly acts. He will always move in accordance with His Word. That should settle the issue of, "You never know what God is going to do." If you believe His Word, you will know He is going to bring you out on top.

*Let us **hold fast** the profession of our faith without wavering; (for He is faithful that promised).*

(Hebrews 10:23 KJV)

Hold fast to the profession of your faith without wavering. This verse is telling us not to doubt, question, or have any suspicion that God does not mean exactly what He says. It means we don't shift over, go in and out, or move up and down. We are steady on the promises of God.

Hold on to the profession of your faith. *Profession* means confession. It is what you are saying in faith. And remember, your faith is based upon God's Word. Romans 10:17 says, "Faith comes by hearing, and hearing by the word of God." And why should we hold fast to the profession of our faith? Because God is faithful to fulfill whatever you are professing from His Word!

The profession of your faith is your confession of God's Word—in faith. This is how you grip your bat, and in baseball, you have to hold on to your bat to hit the home run!

Faithful is He who promised. Faithful is He who has spoken. So what is it that we are holding fast to? What are we gripping with all of our mind, soul, heart, and strength? The profession of His promises—our confession of His Word—because faithful is He who promised. Therefore, hold fast to the confession of your faith in the promises of God, because God always keeps His promises.

> Hold fast to the confession of your faith in the promises of God, because God always keeps His promises.

God promises that "whoever calls on the name of the Lord shall be saved" (Rom. 10:13). When you hold fast to your profession that Jesus Christ is your Lord and Savior, you are saved. Salvation is the first profession of your faith—but not the last!

You should believe and profess all the promises of God, because God fulfills His promises when you believe. Unless you believe them, they will not be fulfilled in your life. You see, God's Word does not return void, but it is not performed in every person's life. There are a lot of people who have rejected and denied God's Word or parts of His Word.

Those who reject God's Word concerning salvation will not see the promised blessing of being born again fulfilled in their lives. Instead, the promises of judgment will be fulfilled in their lives. Furthermore, believers who reject certain promises of God, such as healing, peace, joy, protection, and prosperity, will not receive those blessings. The provisions of God are only performed in the lives of those who mix faith with the Word of God.

We also believe and therefore speak.

(2 Corinthians 4:13)

Say it out loud: WE BELIEVE AND THEREFORE WE SPEAK. What is it we believe? We believe the promises of God and we speak them. We hold fast to that profession without wavering. We hold on to our bat!

Jesus said, "I will never leave you. I will never forsake you." If you are alone and you are professing loneliness, emptiness, and depression, there is a promise that has been left to you, but you may not be inheriting the blessing of it. Why? Because unless you hold fast to that profession of, "Jesus will never leave me; His joy is with me and His peace is inside of me," then that will not be fulfilled in your life. Hold fast to the profession of your faith without wavering, because faithful is He who promised.

Jesus' life was an example to us, particularly in Matthew 4:1-11, when the devil came and tempted Him. With each temptation, Jesus answered, "It is written…," and spoke God's Word that applied to the situation. With each push of the devil to get Him off the promises of God, Jesus came back with another promise, such as, "It is written, 'Man shall not live by bread alone, but by every word that proceeds from the mouth of God'" (Matt. 4:4). What was Jesus doing? He was holding fast to the profession of His faith. He was holding on to the Word of God—the sword of the Spirit.

Above all, taking the shield of faith with which you will be able to quench all the fiery darts of the wicked one. And take the helmet of salvation, and the sword of the Spirit, which is the word of God.

(Ephesians 6:16-17)

We have been talking about the part of your armor that is the shield of faith, which quenches every fiery dart. But another part of your armor is the sword of the Spirit, which is the spoken Word of God you declare with your mouth. You say what God says! In that particular phrase, "the word of God," "word" is the Greek word *rhema*, which means the Word of God spoken, or the spoken Word (W.E. Vine, *Complete Expository Dictionary of Old and New Testament Words*, 1985, p. 683.) When you speak God's Word in faith from your heart, the Word of God becomes the sword of the Spirit.

Just picking up your Bible and waving it at the devil is not going to make him leave any more than just waving your bat around is going to hit the ball. Just having a Bible on the shelf or displaying that big family Bible on your coffee table—you know, the big white one with a picture of Jesus on the front— is not going to send the devil packing any more than leaving your bat in the dugout is going to get you a home run. It is the Word on your lips, the profession of your faith—holding on to your bat—that is going to rebuke and resist the enemy!

We have to understand what Paul is talking about when he tells us to hold fast to the profession of our faith. A good illustration of what *not* to do was when the children of Israel came to the edge of the promised land. God had told them, "I am giving you a land flowing with milk and honey. I will drive out the inhabitants. I will give you fields and storehouses and cities to dwell in." (See Numbers 13:27.) But when the 12 spies came back to report on the land, 10 of them gave an evil report.

When the children of Israel heard that the land had giants in it, and the evil-report guys said, "We were like grasshoppers there," the Israelites began to say, "We would rather go back and die in the wilderness than go into this land." (See Numbers 14:2.) So instead of holding fast to the profession of their faith in God's Word, they professed doubt, fear, and unbelief. They began to profess the opposite of what God had said. (See Numbers 13:31-33.)

What happens when *you* face giants? Do you say, "Ahhhhh…!" Or do you open your mouth and say, "It is written: Christ in me is greater than the giants that I am facing"? (See First John 4:4.) How about when you are home alone at night. Maybe no big giants are threatening you, but you are sitting there and that old loneliness starts creeping in. It is just those four walls and you. Do you profess your feelings? Do you confess the circumstances? Or do you declare, "Jesus, I thank You that You are always with me. You never leave me. You never forsake me. Thank You, Lord, that You are my comfort."

What you say in the moment of trial will either put you over or take you under.

Now you understand, it is one thing to speak God's Word in a church service, but it is really another thing to do it when you are out there facing the battle. When there is a sickness or a disease that comes, do you profess all of the symptoms, all of the facts, all of the reports, and forget about the promises of God? Or in that moment of trial, do you stand up and begin to say, "It is written, by His stripes I am healed. He took my infirmities, bore my sicknesses, and carried my diseases"? (See First Peter 2:24 and Matthew 8:17.)

What you say in the moment of trial will either put you over or take you under. God has given us His Word, His Spirit, His life, His presence, His faith, His joy, and His peace. All of those things have been provided, but until we mix faith with the Word of God and speak accordingly, we will not see His power at work in our lives.

Hebrews 4:2 relates this incident:

For indeed the gospel was preached to us as well as to them; but the word which they heard did not profit them, not being mixed with faith in those who heard it.

The children of Israel did not mix faith with the Word that they heard preached to them. Therefore, it did not profit them.

> ## Until we mix faith with the Word of God and speak accordingly, we will not see His power at work in our lives.

Moses preached the Word directly from God, who said, "They have not rejected you, but they have rejected Me" (1 Sam. 8:7). So when a preacher is preaching the promises—the Word of God, the Word of faith—and someone rejects it, the one who is preaching the message may feel a sense of rejection. But God will say, "They did not reject you. They were really rejecting Me, because you were just delivering My Word."

That is what happened to the children of Israel. The Word came, but there was no profit in it for them. "Profit" means results, the blessings and provisions of God. Instead of mixing faith with God's Word, they mixed it with fear, doubt, and unbelief. So they did not enter into the promised land and profit.

But Joshua the son of Nun and Caleb the son of Jephunneh, who were among those who had spied out the land, tore their clothes; and they spoke to all the congregation of the children of Israel, saying: "The land we passed through to spy out is an exceedingly good land. If the Lord delights in us, then He will bring us into this land and give it to us, 'a land which flows with milk and honey'."

(Numbers 14:6-8)

"But my servant Caleb, because he has a different spirit in him and has followed Me fully, I will bring into the land where he went, and his descendants shall inherit it."

(Numbers 14:24)

There were two spies who stood up with a different spirit. They were still holding onto their bats! Do you have that Joshua and Caleb spirit? God said they had a "different spirit." What was the spirit? It was the spirit of faith, and you and I have the same spirit of faith!

And since we have the same spirit of faith, according to what is written, "I believed and therefore I spoke," we also believe and therefore speak.

(2 Corinthians 4:13)

Oh, I like the spirit of faith! And when Joshua and Caleb told the people they were well able to take the land (see Num. 13:30), the glory of God came in the Tabernacle and God gave witness to the Word that was being spoken. But the people spoke of stoning them! (See Numbers 14:10.) They not only rejected the Word, but also the glory of God that was confirming His Word as a sign and wonder in their midst.

> What you confess will either take you into the land of promise or bury you in the desert.

So God spoke to them as it is recorded in Numbers 14:11,20-23. God said to them, "As truly as you have spoken in My ears, it will be done unto you. All of you who murmured against Me shall go and die in the wilderness. All of you twenty years old and upward, except for My servants, Joshua and Caleb, because they had another spirit." God held them accountable for the words they spoke.

What you confess will either take you into the land of promise or bury you in the desert. The choice is up to you. God has set before us life and death, blessing and cursing—and then, so we do not miss which one to choose, God said, "Choose life." It is a simple choice, but it is amazing how many people miss it because they are moved by their feelings. They get over into the soulish realm of emotions. They are stirred by the opinions of other people.

This is an hour where you cannot fiddle around with your health, your salvation, your loved ones being saved, your joy, your peace, or your victory. It is time to stand on the Word of God, to please God in whatever circumstance you are facing and say, "What does the Word of God say?" What does God say about your finances, your marriage, your children, or whatever?

Some believers are confessing what the situation looks like and what they feel like. They are repeating what the bankers and the talk show "experts" say. But this is a time for you to profess and hold on to the Word of God. Take hold of that bat and don't let go! Then watch God's powerful promises blow your problems right out of the ballpark!

Chapter 7

Faith and Patience to Hit and Run

MANY TIMES A PITCHER throws high or low in an attempt to get the batter to swing at something less than a good pitch. If the batter wants to get a hit badly enough, he or she will take the bait and swing at wild pitches like these. But a skilled batter waits for the right pitch, and sometimes that requires great patience.

Therefore do not cast away your confidence, which has great reward. For you have need of patience.

(Hebrews 10:35-36 KJV)

Say it out loud. PATIENCE. *You* have need of patience! Now, the word *patience* here means "endurance, constancy." (See James Strong, *Greek Dictionary of the New Testament*, #5281.) Simply put, it means staying with it, not quitting, not fainting, not throwing in the towel, and not giving up.

And let us not grow weary while doing good, for in due season we shall reap if we do not lose heart.

(Galatians 6:9)

If you have sown good seeds and you hold on, when the time is right you will reap a great harvest. This means there is a time frame. There is a due season.

Have you been looking for your due season? Maybe you are looking for your due season in your finances, in healing, in the salvation of loved ones, or in reconciliation of relationships in a family. Or are you seeking your due season in victory over an addiction or triumph over a compulsive habit, such as overeating, vain imaginations, or panic attacks?

You must be persistent, steadfast, and constant to obtain God's promises. You must believe, "I will obtain the full reward. I will not stop short with a partial fulfillment of any one of His promises." This means you will step up to bat—believing, receiving, and confessing God's Word—until you hit and score, which is when the full manifestation comes.

> Therefore do not cast away your confidence, which has great reward. For **you have need of endurance** (the King James Version says "patience") so that after you have done the will of God, you may receive the promise.
>
> (Hebrews 10:35-36)

A young man in his late 20s had a cancerous growth in his body, but he was saved and turned on to the Word of God. He only had an eighth-grade education, but he read the Bible and believed every word of it. He refused to get into unbelief. Day after day the pain in his body continued, but he stood on God's Word and believed that the seed of the Word was growing in him at a faster rate than the cancer.

This young man chose over and over again to believe that the input of the Word was pushing the cancer right out of his body. The day came when the growth totally disappeared and he was fully healed. Because he endured, even in the midst of severe pain, he received the reward of God's promise of healing and wholeness.

If you will remain steadfast in believing the Word of God, you will obtain the full promises of God. The promise may be that your mate will accept Jesus Christ and be filled with the Holy Spirit. It may be that a rebellious teenager will come home. It may be that your bills will be paid in full, all of your needs will be met, and you will have money left over to put a greater financial investment into missions. The promise may be for the healing of your body or it may be for living in a continual state of joy. Perhaps you have only received about 30 percent of the promise of Isaiah 51:11:

> So the ransomed of the Lord shall return, and come to Zion with singing, with everlasting joy on their heads. They shall obtain joy and gladness; sorrow and sighing shall flee away.

Hold steady for the full reward of God's promises. He will not deny you. You will obtain the full reward of God's peace as you hold fast to the confession of Jesus' words in John 14:27:

> Peace I leave with you, My peace I give to you; not as the world gives do I give to you. Let not your heart be troubled, neither let it be afraid.

Believe and confess God's Word until you win!

Do not let go of the confession of your faith. Believe and confess God's Word until you win! You can trust God's Word, for God says "yes" to all of His promises. He never says maybe, sometime, or no to His promises. His promises include healing and divine health, deliverance, wholeness, financial prosperity, open doors of opportunity, direction, wisdom—anything of which you have need.

You know, a batter doesn't only need patience to wait for the right pitch. He also needs patience to know when to run. When a batter hits the ball and runs to first base, he doesn't keep on running unless the time is right. If he runs at the wrong time, he will be tagged out.

> Do not be moved by your circumstances or by what you see or hear. Hold fast to God's Word.

Once you lock into a promise of God, do not step off your base until it is safe to reach home plate! In other words, do not be moved until you receive of Him! God says in Hebrews 10:36 that if you will be persistent, you will receive the full reward or the complete manifestation of His promises.

Do not dig up the seed of God's Word that you have planted in your life. That would be like getting a base hit, running to second base, and then running back to first again! Whenever you plant seeds in the natural, there is a germination period before they break through the soil. If you are not persistent in believing that the seed, the soil, the sunshine, and the moisture are doing their job, you will begin to wonder whether the seed is growing, and you will be tempted to dig it up.

When my daughters, Sarah and Ruthie, were younger, they planted seeds for a science fair project. They didn't see sprouts immediately, so they were tempted to dig up the seeds to see if they were growing. Have you ever been tempted to dig up your seed? You know that the Word says that by Jesus' stripes you are healed. (See Isaiah 53:5.) But you prayed, you believed that you received, and waited for the manifestation. You mixed faith with the Word, but it did not break through the ground and manifest immediately. You kept looking at your body, because your body kept saying, "I am sick."

The longer you look at your body and listen to it, the greater the battle with what you believe in your heart. Never confess, "I do not think the Word is working in me. I am not healed. I must have done something wrong." If you have planted the Word in your heart and you are believing and confessing it, you can be confident that it is growing and multiplying.

Confidence is one of the things a ballplayer works on during spring training. The coaches work hard to instill it in the players so that when they get into a game they will not crumble, become confused, or make mistakes under pressure. God's Word works in a similar way. The more of His encouraging Word we read and hear, the more confidence we will have in that Word to work mightily in our lives and circumstances.

Do not be moved by your circumstances or by what you see or hear. Hold fast to God's Word, for according to Jeremiah 1:12, He is faithful to perform His Word. If something does not work, try another route or another direction. There are a lot of different avenues one can use to reach a goal.

Persistence means:
Do not quit moving toward the goal.

Just because you get a base hit instead of a home run doesn't mean you aren't going to score. This is where patience and perseverance come in. This is where listening to the Holy Spirit is vital. He may show you a window of opportunity to run to the next base or tell you to stay put for the moment because the time isn't right. But if you hold onto God's promise and obey His Spirit, you will reach home plate every time!

Perhaps you have a vision of going into a foreign country as a missionary to train the nationals. You have tried it, but it seemingly hasn't worked. That does not mean you should quit; nor does it mean that you are supposed to go back and do exactly what you did before. That is not the part you are to be persistent about. Persistence means: *Do not quit moving toward the goal.*

Sometimes an alteration needs to be made in your method of reaching the goal. If you do not dig up your seed, God's promises will reach full maturity. Remember, you are not limited to nine innings; you play until you win! Some of your harvests are months and years down the road. Not all of them will manifest immediately. Your part is to endure in the game from start to finish, continuing at a steady pace, never yielding to thoughts of doubt and unbelief. Such thoughts will knock you off base and sometimes clear out of the game.

Some of the greatest workers I know are those who work at a continuous, steady pace, as opposed to those who put out an exceptional quantity for short periods of time. Those who are steady day in and day out make the greatest strides. Some people can crank out a lot of work when they set their minds to it, but it is those who are *continually steadfast* who get the job done and obtain the full reward. It is this way with the promises of God. It is getting hold of God's promises for the long haul that counts.

> It is those who are *continually steadfast* who get the job done and obtain the full reward.

As I was meditating on steadfastness, I thought about the yards I used to mow in the summer. I started doing this when I was 11 years old. When Dad left for work in the morning, he would deliver the lawn mower to the location where I was supposed to mow. During the day, I would hop on my bicycle and go mow that yard. Then Dad would pick the mower up again in the evening. I had a good thing going! He bought all the gas and oil, and I kept all the money. It kept me out of trouble, so he thought it was a good deal too.

> Wait for the right pitches, stay on the base when He says, "Stay," and run like crazy when He says, "Go!"

One yard I mowed took four hours. When I started, I would think about all the times down and back, around this tree and around that shrub. After I had worked for about an hour, it looked like I had not done a thing. But if I stayed with it long enough and persisted, I would get the job done.

Have you ever felt that way when believing for the manifestation of God's promises in your life? If you will stay with His promises, ultimately the seed of His Word will come to full maturity in your life. Patience is a necessary ingredient in order for you to stay on course in the race of life. To run with patience means to run with perseverance, endurance, steadfastness, and consistency. James 1:2-4 says the end result of patience is that you will be perfect, complete, and lacking nothing.

There's no other way to hit the right pitch, run the bases, and score a run except through faith and patience. You must trust God by believing His promises to you, and then you must not budge from your belief until you see it come to pass. Wait for the right pitches, stay on the base when He says, "Stay," and run like crazy when He says, "Go!"

Chapter 8

Physical Conditioning

IN ORDER TO HIT curve balls out of the ballpark you must be in good physical condition. Champion hitters will lift weights and work out to be at their best for the regular season games. This kind of physical conditioning is a part of spring training, but it continues throughout the rest of the ballplayer's year. Even during the off season, a ballplayer must continue physical conditioning.

Unfortunately, it is the off season that is the ballplayer's greatest time of temptation. The pressure is off, he's still being paid even though he's not playing or practicing, and it is so easy to let good habits slide. He might get into some bad habits such as eating too much fattening food and getting too little exercise.

Christians have off seasons too. These are those seasons of prosperity and peace that come after great victories. Maybe you finally got out of debt, your family got saved, or you received the full manifestation of a healing. There is great celebration and rejoicing, but then what do you do?

As Christians, we cannot stop training in off seasons, because we cannot afford to be out of shape when a curve ball comes blasting our way. The most devastating injuries occur in the Body of Christ when we become complacent about the things of God because the pressures of life are off for awhile.

Ballplayers are more likely to suffer injuries when they are out of shape, and when an athlete suffers an injury, it usually puts them on the sidelines. It puts them out of the game. Depending on the severity of the injury, it can sometimes mean the end of a career for a professional ballplayer.

It is the same way for Christians. When we experience physical illness and disease in our bodies, we can end up on the sidelines. And if the devil has his way, he will do his best to put us out of the game completely. Jesus told us in John 10:10, "The thief does not come except to steal, and to kill, and to destroy."

The thief Jesus is referring to is the devil. The devil's goal is to steal your health, your financial resources, and your overall productivity. One way he does this is through sickness and disease. But look at the rest of that verse, "I have come that they may have life, and that they may have it more abundantly" (John 10:10).

Jesus is clearly showing us the contrast: God wants us to have lives of health, strength, and abundance. That is His plan for every one of us. Your physical conditioning and the health of your body—how you take care of yourself—can make you more successful against the attacks of the devil.

Whenever someone receives a diagnosis that they have a life-threatening disease or illness, it is a signal that their whole life must change. I believe this point in the healing process is often overlooked by both medical professionals and ministerial leadership. When a critical need for healing is faced, people will give you Scriptures, they will tell you how to release your faith and confess the Word—which are all good. But if your life is going the wrong direction, without a life change you will be sick again. An evaluation beyond the physical arena is needed.

A physical checkup in the natural realm includes an examination of the chemistry of the blood, the vital signs, the heart, and every part of the body. A spiritual checkup is just as comprehensive. It begins with some basic questions and honest responses, such as:

1. How is my relationship with God?

2. How are my relationships with family, friends, and business associates?

3. What is my purpose in life, and am I pursuing that with diligence and integrity?

4. What drives or motivates me?

5. Am I living right?

6. Are my priorities in order?

7. Who am I following throughout my day—God, the devil, or myself?

When people cannot answer these questions satisfactorily, whether they have a life-threatening disease or not, they sometimes take their lives in suicide. That is not God's plan for anyone, for He left a message of hope and purpose for you and me in Jeremiah 29:11 (NIV):

*"For I know the plans I have for you," declares the Lord, "plans to prosper you and not to harm you, plans to give you **hope and a future**."*

A life change begins with repentance, by saying, "Lord, I am sorry that I have not put You and Your Kingdom first." First John 1:9 says:

If we confess our sins, He is faithful and just to forgive us our sins and to cleanse us from all unrighteousness.

Once we repent, we are headed toward the goal of *wholeness—not* just toward being healed physically, but being in the perfect will of God. We are designed so the spirit, soul, and body affect each other. What happens in your body affects your mind. What happens in your mind affects your spirit. What happens in your spirit affects your mind and body. They interact and affect one another.

When a person is not right in their relationship with God, though they are trying to be healed using spiritual truths, internal blockages will stop the flow of God's power from going into them. The obvious ones would be gross sin, immorality, uncleanness, and doing things that are wrong. However, there are also blockages caused by doing things that don't appear to be bad.

The problem might be neglect of spending special, private time with the Lord in prayer and studying His Word. Instead, you are so preoccupied with serving God, you have neglected that intimate time with Him. This is the Martha syndrome. Mary sat at Jesus' feet while Martha was hurried, worried, and bothered because Mary was not helping her. (See Luke 10:38-42.)

Sports are not a bad thing or a sin—unless they take your time away from the Lord, your family, and your church. You see, good things can steal your spiritual well-being in a very subtle way over a period of time. But good or bad, simple repentance is all we need to be free again.

After repentance comes cleansing and joy. That is where we need to be—where nothing within us blocks us from receiving from God. When Paul wrote his first letter to the Corinthians, he confronted the sin in their church. They dealt with it and repented. His second letter to the Corinthians commends them for their repentance. Notice what he says in Second Corinthians 7:9-10:

> Now I rejoice, not that you were made sorry, but that your sorrow led to repentance. For you were made sorry in a godly manner, that you might suffer loss from us in nothing. For godly sorrow produces repentance

leading to salvation, not to be regretted; but the sorrow of the world produces death.

Godly, heartfelt sorrow for sin causes repentance, which produces salvation, healing, and wholeness in every area of your being. Just being sorry you got caught will produce more death. Verse 11 indicates how you know that you have godly sorrow:

> *For observe this very thing, that you sorrowed in a godly manner: What diligence it produced in you, what clearing of yourselves, what indignation, what fear, what vehement desire, what zeal, what vindication! In all things you proved yourselves to be clear in this matter.*
>
> (2 Corinthians 7:11)

A person who has made a true change, whether they have a life-threatening disease or not, will desire God's Word and His Spirit more than anything else in this world. They will go after the things of God and give diligence to them. Godly sorrow and repentance produce diligence.

"What clearing of yourselves...." People will get rid of wrong associations and relationships when they truly repent. Anything that causes them to go the wrong way spiritually, mentally, emotionally, or physically will be dropped from their lives.

"What indignation...." Repentance will cause indignation about sin.

"What fear...." The fear of the Lord is to depart from evil. (See Proverbs 16:6.) A person who has really repented will run from evil.

"What vehement desire...." *Vehement* means intense. A repentant people want Jesus intensely—with all of their being.

"What zeal..." for the things of God. When people have truly repented, you will not have to beg them to go to church. God is the One they are living for, and they want all of Him they can get.

"What vindication! In all things you proved yourselves to be clear in this matter." Godly repentance will cause you to renounce everything that hinders your relationship with Jesus Christ—not because someone tells you to, but because you *want* to.

The cares of the world, the deceitfulness of riches, and the lust for "things" (Mark 4:19) have some people so ensnared—even people in life-threatening illnesses—that they are unable to break free of them in their own efforts. There must be a life change, because even if you recover through medical treatments, unless the patterns of your former lifestyle are changed, you will have recurring illnesses.

Stress, worry, and fear have been documented in many medical journals as being causes of illnesses and diseases. Many life-threatening illnesses (some of the curve balls in life) come after extended periods of intense stress, emotional upheaval, trauma, anger, bitterness, strife, hatred, grief, or sorrow. Heaviness, disappointment, rejection, and loneliness have been added to the causes of life-threatening sicknesses, along with poor diet, insufficient rest, lack of exercise, alcohol, drugs, and cigarettes.

God put within us an immune system to fight off enemy particles in our bodies. This system is designed to destroy destructive germs and negative cells, such as those that cause cancer. The immune system sends out chemicals and positive cells to fight and destroy bad ones. When the immune system is worn down, diseases (enhanced through anger, strife, fear, unforgiveness, bitterness, depression, loneliness, and similar negative emotions) gain inroads into the body.

Here are several life changes you can initiate to bring your spirit, soul, and body into alignment with divine health and wholeness. If you sense you are in need of a little spring training, consider these areas of possible improvement:

1. RESET YOUR PRIORITIES.

Trust in the Lord with all of your heart, and lean not on your own understanding; in all your ways acknowledge Him, and He shall direct your paths.

(Proverbs 3:5-6)

You can make a decision, "Lord, from now on, I am going to let You set my priorities."

2. ADJUST YOUR SCHEDULE.

But seek first the kingdom of God and His righteousness, and all these things shall be added to you.

(Matthew 6:33)

You can decide, "The Kingdom of God is going to be first in my life. I am not going to fast and pray only when the church calls a time of corporate church fasting and prayer. I am going to put prayer at the beginning of my day." Jesus gave us the example of early morning prayer. If the Son of God needed to start His day with prayer, how much more must we need it!

3. RELAX IN FAITH.

Casting all your care upon Him, for He cares for you.

(1 Peter 5:7)

Since the God of Israel neither slumbers nor sleeps, why should you stay awake all night worrying? (See Psalm 121:3-4.) Cast your cares upon the Lord and relax in faith. Once you have given something to Him, do not take it back again. He is well able to handle anything that comes your way.

4. REST IN THE LORD.

There remains therefore a rest for the people of God. For he who has entered His rest has himself also ceased from his works as God did from His.

(Hebrews 4:9-10)

Some people are so uptight they make coffee nervous! You can decide, "Lord, I will rest in You and lean on Your everlasting arms." And do not overlook your need for natural rest. God made our bodies to require regular sleep; it is part of His design. A good night's sleep can go a long way toward relieving stress, increasing mental alertness, and giving you physical stamina for all the tasks of your day.

5. LAUGH.

A merry heart does good, like medicine, but a broken spirit dries the bones.

(Proverbs 17:22)

Many people are standing up on the outside, but they are lying down on the inside. Depression will cause you to lie down on the inside, and it will hinder the proper functioning of your immune system.

Years ago a man by the name of Norman Cousins faced a life-threatening illness. In his study of the immune system, he learned that laughter can energize its function. If the immune system is energized, it can fight off cancer and other negative cells. He got a number of very funny movies, watched them for hours, and literally laughed himself back to health.

Learn to laugh at your own mistakes, and do not be afraid to share the humor with others in a lighthearted way. I have told our congregation the story of the time my wife Sharon was going to bake some Christmas cookies and candies to give to a neighbor. We thought a plate of homemade treats would be a nice way to strengthen our friendship.

A day or two after we decided to do this, I came home on Christmas Eve. There on the kitchen counter was a plate of cookies and candies, all decorated and ready to go. Sharon was not home yet, so I thought, "There they are. I will just take these on over and say hello."

When Sharon got home and I told her what I had done, you should have seen the look on her face. Through gales of laughter, she explained to me that she had not had time to bake anything yet. The plate I had cheerfully delivered to our new neighbors was the very plate of Christmas treats the neighbor had given to Sharon earlier in the day! We have gotten a lot of merry heart medicine over that story!

6. EAT THE RIGHT FOODS.

Replace fried foods (those heavy in fat and high in cholesterol) with fresh vegetables, fruits, and whole grains. Drink plenty of water and ease up on sugary soft drinks that can give you a burst of energy followed by a big letdown. We cannot make a "god" out of eating. It is all right to enjoy food, but we ought to have enough sense to eat things that will not cause health problems.

7. EXERCISE.

In Bible days, Jesus and His disciples did not hop in a chariot when they wanted to go somewhere. They walked everywhere they went. What we call exercise today was their normal way of life. Find exercises you like and stay with them.

Schedule them into your day just like you would an appointment. Our family exercises together when we can, and that way we encourage one another in the habit.

8. Forgive.

On many occasions people have come to the altar asking me to pray for their healing. They have said, "I am a doer of the Word and I speak all the right things, but I have this continual problem." In some cases I have asked, "What is the situation with your father?" They have sometimes answered, "I was abused." I will then ask, "Have you forgiven him?" They have often answered, "No."

You can believe the Word and confess it, but unforgiveness will block the power of God from working in you. It is time to repent and get *all* of the negative-producing enemy activators totally out of your spirit, body, and mind.

By doing what is necessary to get into good physical condition and staying that way even in the off seasons, you will be prepared at any time to meet those curve balls that come your way. You will be alert, ready, and strong enough for the circumstances—and in the end you'll be scoring runs for the Kingdom of God!

Chapter 9

The Winning Strategy

WHEN SPRING TRAINING is over and the new season begins, there are a lot of unknowns for every player. There are over 100 games to play in the regular professional season. No one except God knows the future. Day by day, every player steps out on that field in faith:

1. Faith that he has developed his skills and will be able to give his best,

2. Faith that his teammates will do the same, and

3. Faith that hard work, practice, and training will pay off.

God wants our lives to be based on faith too. When we step out the front door every morning, we do not know all that we will face—and we do not know the outcome of the activities that are scheduled in our day. So we walk by faith, faith that our time of early morning prayer has prepared us for what lies ahead, faith that the Word will work in every circumstance, faith that God will meet our inadequacies with His capabilities, and faith that our heritage in Christ is sufficient to have a victorious day, a victorious week—a victorious life.

*For whatever is born of God overcomes the world.
And this is the victory that has overcome the world—our
faith. Who is he who overcomes the world, but he who
believes that Jesus is the Son of God?*

(1 John 5:4-5)

Every person has the capacity and ability to have faith in God, to trust Him and walk in victory in this life. Romans 12:3 says, "God has dealt to each one a measure of faith." The victory that Jesus won through His death, burial, and resurrection has been transferred to you and me. *Reigning in this life is a gift from God.* Everyone who receives God's grace, mercy, and the gift of righteousness has the right to live in triumph right here on the earth.

First John 5:4 says that faith is the victory. Faith *accepts* what God has done through His Son and makes it a reality. We *believe* it on the inside of us, then we *declare* it with our lips and *act on it*. We *practice* it. We *obey* what the Word of God says to do and trust God to perform it.

But how does faith work? We can compare faith to a car, which is capable of transporting you wherever you need to go. However, without gasoline in the tank, you will not go very far. In a similar way, the love of God is what causes your faith to work. Galatians 5:6 says faith works by *love*. In other words, faith is fueled by love.

> Everyone who receives God's grace, mercy, and the gift of righteousness has the right to live in triumph right here on the earth.

In a baseball game, especially in the outfield, it is essential for the players to work as a team. There has to be cooperation and unity. The more the players can think and act in unison, the more successful they are on the field. This is the winning strategy: teamwork.

> ## The love of God
> ## is what causes your faith to work.

Paul said if you have faith to move mountains but you do not have love, it will not profit you. Many people have great faith, and they understand the principles of faith. They know the benefits of Christ's death, burial, and resurrection. They know the Holy Spirit is in them. They know Jesus has seated them with Him at the right hand of God the Father and they are heirs of God and joint-heirs with Jesus. Many people have a good start in faith, but suddenly things stop. They begin to wonder, "Why isn't it working anymore? I still believe and confess the same things, but it is not producing results."

God is calling them to a higher level of faith, a more powerful working of faith, and it is based upon His love. Love is one of the most important issues to settle regarding the operation of faith.

> *He who says he is in the light, and hates his brother, is in darkness until now. He who loves his brother abides in the light, and there is no cause for stumbling in him. But he who hates his brother is in darkness and walks in darkness, and does not know where he is going, because the darkness has blinded his eyes.*
>
> (1 John 2:9-11)

In other words, whoever has hatred or ill will toward another person is still in darkness. To be *in the light* means to have revelation and clear perception. Whoever says he is a Christian but continues to hate or despise another person is in darkness and is in deception.

I began to think about how many churches and people across America say they are Christians, yet have prejudice against people of different races, nationalities, and colors. They have so much hatred and prejudice that they say, "We do not want those folks coming into our church. We are not going to have them in this business, in this school, or in this place." Yet, these same people go to church and sing wonderful hymns to God!

You may say, "I love the Lord, but I just cannot stand so-and-so." Let's be honest! You do not love the Lord if you hate your brother or sister! Loving Jesus means loving *all* people, regardless of where they live, their socioeconomic status, educational attainments, color, or nationality. We are called to love every person, because the love of God has been poured into our hearts.

> *Now hope does not disappoint, because the love of God has been poured out in our hearts by the Holy Spirit who was given to us.*
>
> (Romans 5:5)

John compared the love of God to being in a room where there is a lot of light. You do not stumble around when you have the light. You are able to see where you are going. He who loves is walking in the light, and there is no opportunity, reason, or cause for stumbling, error, or sin.

When you walk in hatred, you walk in darkness and cannot see where you are going. Because you are blinded, you will stumble and get into trouble. Some people cannot seem to get loosed from certain sins. Usually, it is because of the hate, bitterness, strife, resentment, and unforgiveness toward someone that is inside of their own heart.

Can you imagine a ball team whose players hated one another? Now imagine a ball team where each member loved one another. Which team do you think would be more likely to succeed? Which team would be able to hit more curve balls?

When I was playing football in a state college, one upperclassman seemed to take a great disliking to me. I do not know what bothered him about me, but he was rough. I would speak to him and he would just glare at me. Without realizing it, I got into the same spirit toward him, even though I already had accepted Jesus Christ. If he was going to glare at me, I decided I would just glare at him.

When I did that, however, my spirit went "tilt!" I got depressed and discouraged over it, and immediately the Holy Spirit let me know, "That is not you. You are different. You are supposed to love him and forgive him."

Suddenly, I saw past what was inside of that guy and realized that he had problems in his own life. He had come from a broken home, and he was acting out of the bitterness and rejection in his own heart. If we get into bitterness and strife, we lose the peace and blessing of God.

When Sharon and I began to travel in ministry, we went to Camden, Arkansas. While we were there, we received a phone call from this same young man. He had been saved and was now heading up the Fellowship of Christian Athletes program in the public school there. He asked me to come speak to them!

When my friend introduced me to his F.C.A. group, he said, "When we were on the college team together, I was always inspired by Billy Joe. I really looked up to him." I thought, "You have got to be kidding!" But what he was talking about was Jesus Christ inside of me.

When someone acts mean to you, they may be going through a war in their own heart and mind. If you take on the same spirit they have, you can be snared into a trap that will pull you down.

Many people today are addicted to drugs and alcohol because their bitterness from emotional hurts was an open door to addiction. In their anger and anguish, their walls fell down, and alcohol and drugs walked right in and conquered them. Many people have fallen into immorality, pornography, perversion, profanity, violence, or compulsive gambling for the same reason.

> Those who are "forgivers," who walk in love and mercy, will walk in victory.

The problem appears to be a horrible vice, but that vice is only the thing that people can see—like the "leaves" of a tree. The root that is causing the problem is really bitterness deep in their heart. Until the root is dealt with, they may stop one sin only to get trapped by another form of evil. That is what happens when a person does not get free on the *inside*.

The person who walks in the light will not stumble, but the person who walks in darkness will stumble over the smallest thing. As an example of being in darkness, when Sharon and I preached in a meeting in Texas some time ago, we stayed up until after midnight to fellowship. We had to be at the airport for a 6 A.M. flight back to Tulsa, so we set our alarm for 5 A.M.

When the alarm went off, it sounded too much like the smoke alarm that awakened me when we had a fire in our home years ago. The hotel was a strange place, and we had not left any lights on. When I first jumped out of bed, I did not know where I was. But I was going to get out of there and make a way for my wife, so I tried to run through the wall! I was tearing into the wall, trying to get through it. Sharon grabbed me and said, "We are okay, Honey. There's no fire."

You may be in darkness, trying to go through a "wall" because there is bitterness and resentment on the inside of you. James 3:14-16 says:

> But if you have bitter envy and self-seeking in your hearts, do not boast and lie against the truth. This wisdom does not descend from above, but is earthly, sensual, demonic. For where envy and self-seeking exist, confusion and every evil thing are there.

In other words, when you get into bitterness, strife, hatred, or unforgiveness, the lights go out. It gets dark and every kind of evil thing can happen in this type of atmosphere.

In working with teenagers who have been involved in drugs, alcohol, or immorality, I have discovered that usually at the core of their problems is bitterness in their heart. They are bitterly hurt and disappointed about something that has happened in the home, either they have been mistreated, they have been abandoned, or their parents are divorced or separated. Rarely does a young person go into immorality, drugs, or alcohol who does not have bitterness in his or her heart. Why? Because bitterness is like AIDS. Although AIDS breaks down the physical immune system, bitterness breaks down the spiritual immune system.

You can have on the helmet of salvation, the breastplate of righteousness, the belt of truth, the gospel of peace, and all your spiritual armor, but without the love of God, it will not work. Those who are "forgivers," who walk in love and mercy, will walk in victory.

The cornerstone of a winning strategy is to make the decision: "I am going to walk in love. I'm going to be a support and encouragement to my team. I'm going to cooperate with them. And I'm going to do my part, for God and for the other players."

Then you can see clearly when that pitcher turns his wrist slightly to release a powerful curve ball. Hallelujah! You will be ready for it and knock it over the fence!

Chapter 10

Taking Charge

ONE OF THE KEYS to playing your best in sports is to play with confidence. Some people yield to fear, self-doubt, insecurity, concern for what the spectators think, etc., and it ruins their performance on the field. You have to remember your training, physical conditioning, practicing, and what your coaches have told you, and then get control of yourself in the game. You have to stay alert, aware of what is happening in the game and ready to deal with anything that comes your way.

It is time for you to take charge of your spiritual life the same way. One of the devil's tactics is to make people believe they have no choice in the direction of their lives. Having no voice in your own affairs is like playing a baseball game without knowing where the bases are!

If you believe you have no choice in matters pertaining to your life, then when things like a divorce come along, you will buy it with no questions asked. When calamity comes along, you will accept it. When sickness comes, you will receive it. This is not God's will!

There are things you can do to cause God's favor to come your way and reverse the negative situations in your life. *God wants you to be in control of your own life.* Some people have had the mistaken idea that God will take over their life and run it like a robot! The only one I know who takes charge of other people's lives like that is the devil. He desires to take away your will with drugs, alcohol, immorality, mind science religions, deceit, and seduction. Once your will is out of the way, the devil can manipulate and control you as he wills.

> Having no voice in your own affairs is like playing a baseball game without knowing where the bases are!

But God wants your will to be submitted to *His* will! He wants you to take charge of your life. You are not on a runaway horse! The reins are not dragging the ground. It is time for you to grab hold of the reins and cause the situations you are facing to go the way they are supposed to go!

When Sharon and I were first married, we moved into a little garage apartment that we leased for $65 a month, all bills paid. That fall, I got hold of some reading material that was about "the coming economic crash." It told how there were going to be terrible, oppressive times in America. It was built around a spiritual thought, so it seemed to me that it was likely to happen.

The book said there would be so little food that there would be roving gangs of people trying to get something to eat. It would be a frightening time. People would have their houses broken into just so people could steal food.

I got to reading that book and I started believing it. I began thinking, "This is going to happen anytime." We did not have a lot of things, two director's chairs and a pole lamp, but you know, you still want to keep your stuff! When you get to thinking on negative things like that, your imagination can go wild.

And many people live in fear of things that are never going to happen.

Why do so many people have such long faces? Many times they are depressed, discouraged, and have so little energy because they are carrying the weight of the world. If you were carrying the weight of the world, you would look that way, too! But do you know what? Jesus can carry it. The Bible says, even "the government will be upon His shoulder" (Isa. 9:6). So cast that burden on Him!

After reading the book, I said to Sharon, "The book says if you are going to have something to eat, you have to gather up nuts." (The kind that fall out of the trees!) We did not have a lot of money, but I kept a good record of the money we did spend that whole first year of our marriage. My dad was an accountant, my mother was an accountant, and both my brothers were accountants, so I did my best.

I had it budgeted out where we ate on just over $13 a week. How do you do that? Well, you buy one pack of wieners and you eat about one a day. And when you eat it, you slice it and lay it on bread. So we had wiener sandwiches. We also had tuna once a week, a small roast, and macaroni, beans, and potatoes. We had chicken once a week, some poor little chicken that had its legs tied together with a rubber band. But it was fun cooking. And I was so excited to be married to Sharon that every time I sat down to eat, I would spill something!

It is time for you to grab hold of the reins and cause the situations you are facing to go the way they are supposed to go!

Anyway, I told Sharon that we had to be ready before this economic disaster hit because when gangs started roving the streets, there was not going to be any time to go looking for food. Someone else would have already gotten all the nuts gathered up! I was convinced of this, so we bought all the dried beans we could find (all that we could afford on our $13-a-week budget). We put the beans in a canister, but I knew it was not enough to last us very long.

Then I thought about a park located near where we lived. That park had a lot of good nut trees. So I told Sharon we would each take a sack and go down to the park. Sharon said, "We are going to do *what*?"

"We are going to gather nuts, Honey. I know you haven't read this book, but just trust me." So we headed for the park with our sacks. We were making sure we got those nuts before anybody else did.

Sharon said later that even the squirrels did not want the nuts we were gathering. I had grown up going hunting and doing things outdoors, but I had never thought much about eating wild nuts or anything like that. What we were gathering were acorns. So we filled our two sacks and took them home to store. But before we put them away, I thought, "Well, I ought to try these." I knew enough to know that most nuts taste better if you roast them. So I turned on the oven and roasted them for awhile, then I let them cool off.

I can still remember taking one of those nice big, juicy acorns and biting into it. It was terrible! And I got a revelation. The revelation was, *There has got to be something better than this!* It hit me that I had gotten underneath the circumstances—in fear—living in torment when God was calling us to reign in this life.

The God who made manna has provided for Sharon and me and our family all through the years. And we have seen that fear of what the devil may do is a snare. Your mind starts working overtime trying to figure out the devil's strategy. Not one bad thing may have happened, but he gets you tied in knots thinking about what *might* happen. And like that book's effect on me, you can get a little *nutty*!

Instead of worrying about something bad happening, I began to realize, "we are seated with Christ in heavenly places" (Eph. 2:6). Then I thought of First Corinthians 15:57, which says, "But thanks be to God, who gives us the victory through our Lord Jesus Christ." We are not *trying* to get the victory. Because we are His, we already *have* the victory!

I thought of what David the psalmist said: "I have been young, and now am old; yet I have not seen the righteous forsaken, nor his descendants begging bread" (Ps. 37:25). Second Corinthians 2:14 says, "Now thanks be to God who always leads us in triumph in Christ." God wants to reveal His *triumph* in our lives—not defeat and failure.

When Paul and Silas were in prison, they began to sing praises to God, and He shook the prison. The Lord wants to shake the prison of doubt, fear, and uncertainty that has tried to knock you down, but it will take praise, thanksgiving, and a revelation: "Everything is going to be all right. God will take care of me." What a difference it makes when you realize, "I am not trying to get the victory. I have the victory."

> While every circumstance and situation, feeling, or even world events are subject to change, God's Word is unchanging.

When I was at O.R.U., the chaplain at that time would ask me every time he saw me, "Billy Joe, do you have the victory?" "Yeah, Brother Bob, I've got the victory." Two or three days later when I would see him on campus, he would ask, "Billy

Joe, have you got the victory?" "No, Brother Bob, I don't have the victory." I was on a roller coaster with my feelings according to how things were going—and I was often underneath the circumstances.

I have since learned—regardless of world events, feelings, or the circumstances around me—to be moved *only by God's Word!* While every circumstance and situation, feeling, or even world events are subject to change, God's Word is unchanging. "Forever, O Lord, Your word is settled in heaven" (Ps. 119:89).

> By taking charge of your feelings, thoughts, and circumstances, you can play your best in the game of life and serve God in a powerful way.

By taking charge of your feelings, thoughts, and circumstances, you can play your best in the game of life and serve God in a powerful way. You won't just react to things around you, but you will be in control. When what you thought was a straight pitch begins to curve, you will not be moved by what you see. You will be moved by the Word of God and led by the Holy Spirit. And you will know exactly what to do!

Chapter 11

Throw the Devil Out of the Game!

ONE OF THE MOST important people in a baseball game is not a player at all. He is the umpire. He has authority. His word carries power. He knows the rules of the game and he enforces them. If a player or a coach tries to argue with the umpire, he can throw them out of the game!

You may have never thought about it this way, but you and I are supposed to be umpires over our own lives through the power of Jesus that is within us. In fact, *The Amplified New Testament* uses these words:

> *And let the peace (soul harmony which comes) from Christ rule (act as umpire continually) in your hearts (deciding and settling with finality all questions that arise in your minds, in that peaceful state) to which as (members of Christ's) one body you were also called (to live). And be thankful (appreciate), (giving praise to God always).*

> (Colossians 3:15 AMP)

In the summer of 1980 I was flying a private plane back to Tulsa from a ten-year high school reunion in Magnolia, Arkansas. I was inexperienced and made a terrible mistake by flying into a storm. Getting into clouds without an instrument rating is very dangerous!

As I was plunging toward the ground with the plane out of control, the Spirit of God rose up in me and I began to yell, "You're going to make it! Get control of the plane!"

My senses suddenly cleared, and I saw how to level the plane and fly through the clouds. To this day I am amazed that I survived! God helped me do what seemed impossible for me at that moment.

If you feel you are in the clouds and heading for a crash, take charge with the Word of God. Just as I kept yelling to myself, "Do what the instruments are telling you," during my crisis on that flight, you may have to yell at yourself, "Do what the Word is telling you!" The Word of God is your instrument panel that will fly you through the storm.

> If you feel you are in the clouds and heading for a crash, take charge with the Word of God.

Through God's Word, you know that in Christ you have been raised up above the circumstances. As long as you declare that the problems are on top of you, that is exactly where they will stay. But if you will believe God's Word that He already has given you the victory, God will begin to explode His wisdom and power in your life.

As you begin to assume the authority God has given to you and declare, "I have the victory," you will enforce satan's defeat. Tell the devil he is "Out!" You have that right. You have that power. The devil has been defeated, but you have to enforce it every day in your life. Otherwise, he will come back with lies and try to regain a position on top of you. He will ride roughshod over you, trying to convince you that you must play the game by his rules. No way! Throw him out of the game!

Tell the devil he is "Out!" You have that right.

In a normal baseball game, although a particular rule may be allowed, if you do not take advantage of it and act upon it, it will not benefit you. For example, a team can put in a pinch hitter to substitute for one of its regular batters. They might do that because the regular batter has an injured ankle and it will be tough for him to run the bases. Or maybe the pinch hitter is known to have better success against the particular pitcher who is on the mound. Taking advantage of the rule that allows pinch hitters has the potential to help the team win.

Playing by God's rules will help you win too. You can overcome every challenge you face. When you reign in this life, you can give yourself in service to others because you are not trying to become somebody. Many people are trying to be somebody, instead of realizing, "I am already seated together with Christ. I can submit myself totally to God and serve other people. I can play by God's rules, be a winner, and help others win too."

Playing by God's rules will help you win.

When you know who you are in Christ, you will be free to be what God has called you to be. Never again will you be *under* your circumstances! Instead, you will reign over *all* of

95

the circumstances you face from your position in heavenly places in Christ. You will continually enforce satan's defeat as you believe God's Word, speak it from your mouth, and become a doer of it.

> When you know who you are in Christ, you will be free to be what God has called you to be.

Perhaps your business has gone sour and you think there is nothing you can do about it. I am announcing that *you* can take charge. You are the umpire and you can make the call. You can make a change. Perhaps the devil has told you to commit suicide—that there is no reason for you to go on. Today is your day to take charge of the direction of your life through the Holy Spirit. In Christ Jesus, there is hope for you.

Many times the devil will say, "You cannot possibly take control because of your environment, background, or heredity." That is not true! Nothing is impossible with God. You can take charge! In Jesus' name, you can break generational ties that are ungodly. You can change your desires, emotions, and feelings. Sometimes people who are caught up in immoral situations say, "I just cannot help it." Yes, you can! You can take charge and turn your life around today! You can tell your mind and body

> Today is your day to take charge of the direction of your life through the Holy Spirit.

which direction to go: "I am going the way of God's Word, in Jesus' name."

James 4:7 says, "Therefore submit to God. Resist the devil and he will flee from you." Without *first* submitting to God, you will have no power to resist the devil. God is a God of precision. He is a God of vision. He is a God who ordains things to happen for good. We must fight those things that oppose God's direction and vision for our lives.

If you have lost your sense of direction, it is time for you to take charge. Make a commitment to take charge right now by saying: *"I take control of my life under the anointing of the Holy Spirit, in agreement with the Word of God. I will not be tossed about by the whims of the devil. In Jesus' name, I command the devil to leave and I throw him out of my life now!"*

> We must fight those things that oppose God's direction and vision for our lives.

Throwing the devil out of your life will eliminate distractions, discouragement, and problems. You will be free to play your best in the game of life—and increase your batting success!

Chapter 12

Getting Back Up to Bat

SOMETIMES IN A BASEBALL GAME, a batter is hit by the ball thrown by the pitcher. Usually it is just a glancing blow, but sometimes it can be a direct hit. Often it can be very painful, especially in the major leagues! Usually these incidents are accidents, but some pitchers have even been accused of throwing at a batter on purpose.

If you have ever seen someone knocked down, you probably realized he or she might not want to get back up there for another pitch! Getting back up again to play some more can be a challenge in any sport, but particularly if you've just been hurt and are still in pain.

Perhaps you have been knocked down by overwhelming circumstances. You are lying there watching the race of life go by, paralyzed by fear. It is time to get up! In the realm of the Spirit, there are people watching you from Heaven's grandstands. They can see what is going on in your life spiritually.

Therefore we also, since we are surrounded by so great a cloud of witnesses, let us lay aside every weight, and the sin which so easily ensnares us, and let us run with endurance the race that is set before us.

(Hebrews 12:1)

99

Perhaps you have been knocked out of the race because of the hypocrisy of Christians, someone has failed you, or you have fallen because of sin. You have said, "What is the use of getting up? What is the use of going on?" The people in Heaven's grandstands are cheering for you to get up!

> You may be lying down,
> but you do not have to lose the race.

One of the greatest illustrations of this type of situation was in the movie, *Chariots of Fire*, where a young man was deliberately knocked off the running track by his opponent. Lying there, he had a choice to remain off the track or get up and go again. He got up and went on to win the race.

You may be lying down, but you do not have to lose the race. Jesus, the Author and Finisher of the race, will pick you up, put you in the race, and help you finish your course! Don't let go of your dreams and visions because it seems too tough to keep running. Let Jesus help you rise above your pain, wounds, and all the overwhelming circumstances. God is saying, "Get back in the race!"

Maybe you have gone through brokenness in a relationship. You are standing up on the outside, but *inside* you are lying down. God is saying, "Get back up." Possibly you have been deliberately and maliciously wounded or rejected by others. In spite of what you have experienced, the Word of the Lord is, "Get up and get back in the race."

It is time to get your eyes off of why you fell and to stop focusing on your mistakes. It is time to lay aside the weights of past failures and sins and place your focus back on Jesus, the Author and Finisher of your faith. Come out of the dugout and into the Sonshine!

At some time in life, everyone faces struggles, trials, obstacles, oppression, feelings of hopelessness, uselessness, ugliness, and failure that make them feel like they cannot make it. I am sure you have gone through times when you felt like quitting and not going on one more day. I am not referring to giving up where you want to take your own life and die. I am referring to the situations that arise and seem to overwhelm you, such as financial crisis or family problems.

Outwardly, everything appears to be okay, but inwardly you have given up. You have lost hope. Outwardly, you indicate that all is well, but inwardly you feel like it is all over.

Not only is this message for you, but it is also for all those with whom you come in contact. You will come across people in your job, business, office, school, and neighborhood who are ready to give up on life, ready to give up on what they are called to do, ready to quit believing God, or ready to lie down on the inside and just let the world go by. Tell them, *"You can make it!"*

The summer before Sharon and I were married, when I was serving as a youth minister, I found myself in a circumstance that made me feel like I couldn't make it. However, there was one mother in that church who was sensitive to the Spirit of God. She would call me and say, "You can make it!" She gave me the following Scripture from Second Corinthians 4:8-18 (TLB), which ministered to me. I believe it will also minister to you.

We are pressed on every side by troubles, but not crushed and broken. We are perplexed because we don't know why things happen as they do, but we don't give up and quit. We are hunted down, but God never abandons us. We get knocked down, but we get up again and keep going. These bodies of ours are constantly facing death just as Jesus did; so it is clear to all that it is only the living Christ within (who keeps us safe). Yes, we live under constant danger to our lives because we serve the Lord, but this gives us constant opportunities to show forth the power of Jesus Christ within our dying bodies. Because of our preaching we face death, but it has resulted in eternal life for you. We boldly say what we believe (trusting God to care for us), just as the Psalm writer did when he said, "I believe and therefore I speak." We know that the same God who brought the Lord Jesus back from death will also bring us back to life again with Jesus, and present us to Him along with you. These sufferings of ours are for your benefit. And the more of you who are won to Christ, the more there are to thank Him for His great kindness, and the more the Lord is glorified. That is why we never give up. Though our bodies are dying, our inner strength in the Lord is growing every day. These troubles and sufferings of ours are, after all, quite small and will not last very long. Yet this short time of distress will result in God's richest blessing upon us forever and ever! So we do not look at what we can see right now, the troubles all around us, but we look forward to the joys in heaven which we have not yet seen. The troubles will soon be over, but the joys to come will last forever.

Paul was attacked with stones, shipwrecked, beaten with rods, rejected, and thrown into prison; yet he referred to his difficulties as "light afflictions!" Like Paul, you may be surrounded with problems on every side, but if you will receive the Word of God and the ministry of the Holy Spirit, your inner man will stand up and be strong against the obstacles that are attempting to overwhelm you.

When a man's spirit is broken, there is no help. Proverbs 18:14 says, "The spirit of a man will sustain him in sickness, but who can bear a broken spirit?" That same verse in The Living Bible says, "A man's courage can sustain his broken body, but when courage dies, what hope is left?" Paul said that though the outer man may be under attack, the inner man is being renewed day by day. Your inner man is being strengthened daily as you read the Word and fellowship with the Father, Son, and Holy Spirit. This fellowship will bring you living water on a daily basis.

You may feel like you have been knocked down, beaten, drug around, and left for dead. You may not feel like continuing in the game. You may not even want to live another day. You are not alone. Many people feel that way. Many Christians feel that way or have already been through the same experience.

> Today is your day to make
> a quality decision to persevere.

Today is your day to make a quality decision to persevere. Say, "I will not quit. I will step up to bat again. I will play until I win, because the Greater One dwells in me. He will put me over. He will make me a success. I will hold steady and play until I win, because Jesus already won the complete victory for me. I am not a quitter! There is no defeat in me! I am a winner, and I will score in the game of life for Jesus Christ!"

Chapter 13

A Winning Attitude

BACK IN 1962, a new baseball expansion franchise started in New York in the National League. Officially, the team's name was the Metropolitans, but they quickly became known as the Mets. The Mets played so badly that it actually endeared them to their fans.

People showed up by the thousands to cheer them on even though they were losing so many games. They ended their first major league season with a record-setting 40 wins and 120 losses! From 1962 to 1968, the highest they ever finished in the National League East Division was 9th place. But 1969 would be a different story.

In 1969, the Mets started young pitchers named Tom Seaver, Jerry Koosman, and Nolan Ryan, plus a relief pitcher named Tug McGraw. When the regular season had ended, the team that everyone had previously poked fun at won the National League pennant! But even then, very few gave the Mets a chance to win against the Baltimore Orioles in the World Series. The Mets were like David in the Bible; the Orioles were like Goliath. And like David facing the Philistine giant, the Mets had the right attitude—a winning attitude. In only five games, the New York Mets won the 1969 World Series!

The Mets' winning attitude and strategy was based on great pitching and having players who did not give up in the face of formidable odds. David's winning attitude and strategy were based on five principles of victory that are just as valid for us today as they were when the future king of Israel stood against Goliath.

Like the Mets, David was ridiculed for even thinking he could win. Even worse, the taunts were coming from David's own brothers, who accused him of deserting his work as a shepherd just to see the armies in battle. In fact, David was being obedient—taking supplies to his brothers as his father had asked.

David's winning strategy was based on obeying God and fixing his eyes firmly on the power of God, not the appearance of the circumstances. The principles David used to defeat Goliath in his day are just as valid for us today in defeating our giants. The same enemy comes, and the same principles of victory must be applied. Here are the five principles of victory that David used to whip his giant:

1. DAVID MADE TIME TO KNOW GOD.

David had a personal relationship with God. He knew Him. He walked and talked with Him, and he sang songs to the Lord on those hillsides as he tended his father's sheep. Seventy-three of David's songs are recorded in the Psalms. One of them is Psalm 23. "The Lord is my shepherd; I shall not want" (Ps. 23:1). David knew what it was to sit at a table prepared for him in the presence of his enemies. He declared, "Surely goodness and mercy shall follow me all the days of my life" (Ps. 23:6).

Another of David's songs is recorded in Psalm 103. This Psalm also indicates that David had a personal relationship with God.

> *Bless the Lord, O my soul, and forget not **all His benefits:** who forgives all your iniquitles, who heals all your*

diseases, who redeems your life from destruction, who crowns you with lovingkindness and tender mercies, who satisfies your mouth with good things, so that your youth is renewed like the eagle's.

(Psalm 103:2-5)

The big difference between Israel's soldiers and David was that the soldiers knew *about* God, but David *knew* God. David spent time with God—and faith is birthed out of relationship. Some people think relationship with God is built by rules, rituals, and formulas, but your faith in God grows as you become better acquainted with Him.

2. DAVID UNDERSTOOD GOD'S COVENANT

David understood that God is holy and that He is totally committed to those who love and obey Him. That means everything God has and everything He is will be available to the one with whom He is in covenant. That is why it shocked David that no one stepped forward to challenge Goliath.

David understood that a challenge against him was a direct challenge to Almighty God. If you are in covenant with God, the challenges you face are against God Almighty. When you are born again, God is linked up with you, and He will fight for you.

When you understand covenant, then you will not be thinking about how big an illness is. Instead, you will be thinking about how great the Healer is!

WHEN LIFE THROWS YOU A CURVE

Though David was just a teenager, he focused on how big God was, while the rest of Israel's army focused on how big Goliath was. He rose up and challenged Goliath, because he knew Goliath could not prevail against God. If you are facing a giant, something in you needs to rise up and say, "Who is this giant of sickness, disease, sin, strife, or fear trying to rise up against Almighty God?" Is Jesus Christ really in you, or is that just a nice idea? Is the Greater One living in you, or is it just something you sing about?

The whole tribe of Israel heard the same thing David heard, but to them it was just head knowledge, while to David it was heart knowledge. All the Israelites were covenant people, but only one in the bunch (young David) understood it and believed it.

When you understand covenant, then you will not be thinking about how big an illness is. Instead, you will be thinking about how great the Healer is! You will not be thinking about how many problems you have, but what a great Problem Solver you have. When you are in covenant, you know God is committed to you, even to the point of the death of His Son. Romans 8:31-32 says:

> *What then shall we say to these things? If God is for us, who can be against us? He who did not spare His own Son, but delivered Him up for us all, how then shall He not with Him also freely give us all things?*

It is time to be fully persuaded that what God has promised, He is able to perform.

3. DAVID SPOKE HIS FAITH

David spoke his faith out loud in the face of the lies of the devil. If you are going to slay giants, you will have to talk in faith. The giants will speak too! Sickness will say, "I am going to take you out of this life." Financial bondage will say, "I am going to bury you with bankruptcy." Strife and problems in the home will say, "I am going to rip your home and marriage apart."

The Word of God must rise up from within your spirit and come out of your lips with, "It is written," which is the example Jesus gave us for resisting the devil in Matthew 4:1-11. In the face of sickness and disease, you will declare in the words of Psalm 118:17, "It is written, *I shall not die, but live, and declare the works of the Lord.*"

Faith has a language all its own, and the ring of authority can be heard in hell when it is inside your spirit and you speak it out. The devil left Jesus because He spoke with authority. It is time to be fully persuaded that what God has promised, He is able to perform. Believe Him! Speak His promises! Act as if they are already so! David did not have a sword in his hand, but there was a sword in his mouth—the Word of the Living God! Hallelujah!

4. DAVID USED WHAT HE HAD

You may think, "I do not have enough to fight my battle." You have got enough and it is in your hands. As David faced his battle with Goliath, he looked beyond the swords, spears, and javelins and said, "Give me my sling!" He was not intimidated by Goliath. Would God put you in the earth, give His Son for you, raise Him from the dead, and then not supply you with enough to defeat the giants that are in your land?

The word is near you, in your mouth and in your heart, (that is, the word of faith which we preach).

(Romans 10:8)

> Would God put you on the earth, give His Son for you, raise Him from the dead, and then not supply you with enough to defeat the giants that are in your land?

God has given you enough. It is in your hands. Your giant-defeating ability is as close as your breath—the Word of God spoken from your mouth! He will perform His Word when you speak it and believe it.

5. DAVID STARTED SMALL

David learned how to battle the giant by fighting the lion and the bear. What David learned in fighting the lion prepared him to defeat the bear, and what he learned fighting both of them prepared him to whip the giant. Many people want to take on a giant when they would not even take on a kitty cat. They are intimidated by a "meow"!

Let us look at this fifth principle in greater depth. In 1981, we first began our church. We started a small Christian school and Bible institute. We needed a larger facility to house these areas of ministry. We purchased a car dealership on ten acres of land with 66,000 square feet of floor space for $3.3 million with debt that eventually went to 15 percent interest. I had heard about not getting into debt, but I did not take it seriously.

But then the debt hovered over us and oppressed us, saying, "If you do not whip me, you are going to serve me." We fell into debt service. Proverbs 22:7 says, "The borrower is servant to the lender," and we fell into that trap as a ministry. We were in oppressive debt. It was bondage to our lives and it nearly destroyed the ministry in those first few months.

Besides the oppression of debt, we outgrew the remodeled auto mart within just a few months, with no place to go. I learned very quickly what it means to be the tail instead of the head!

> Now it shall come to pass, if you diligently obey the voice of the Lord your God, to observe carefully all His commandments which I command you today, that the Lord your God will set you high above all nations of the earth. And all these blessings shall come upon you and overtake you, because you obey the voice of the Lord your God.
>
> (Deuteronomy 28:1-2)

One of these blessings listed in Deuteronomy 28:13 is:

> And the Lord will make you the head and not the tail; you shall be above only, and not be beneath, if you heed the commandments of the Lord your God.

We made all of our payments in the three and a half years we were in the remodeled auto mart, but it was extremely difficult. After only a few months, I began to cry out to the Lord, "What do we do?" God spoke to me out of First Samuel 17. This story is so real to me because we have lived it. We have been in that same Valley of Elah with the giant of debt challenging us, with everything Sharon and I owned on the line. I mean, they had us hook, line, sinker, boat, motor, boots, and everything! Though we went into slavery, I made a decision, "No more!"

I made a commitment that we would never borrow another dime in the ministry, and I finally got it down in my spirit that we would get out of debt. We would buy land and build with cash. We would be the head and not the tail for the glory of God!

Though some 3,000 years existed between David's challenge and ours, the issue was the same. We faced something so much bigger than us. As I sought the Lord, He spoke, "You haven't whipped the lion and the bear yet. For you, to take on being a debt-free ministry, buying land without debt and building with cash is your giant. But you are trying to take the whole thing on at once."

I said, "Lord, what is our lion? What is our bear?"

Our lion was to get an interim site so we could move out of the auto mart. Our bear would be to sell the auto mart. We needed to move before we sold it so we would not lose the ministry we had. If we moved into another facility before we sold the auto mart, that meant we would be making double payments, so we were trusting it would sell quickly.

God spoke to me about leasing a junior high school building for an interim site. It would house our 750 Christian school students, the Victory Bible Institute students, and our ministry offices.

I made a total of seven personal approaches to the local school officials to lease that building. They did not want to lease it. Instead, they wanted it to sell because of the needs they faced. On the seventh approach to the school, the door opened to lease that junior high building and we moved in during September of 1984.

In fighting our lion, I learned, "Do not give up!" Just because the door looks closed does not mean it will stay closed. Just keep persevering, pressing, knocking, and doing all you know to do. If it does not work one way, try it another way. Many times people knock just one time, or they try just one thing in a battle. They say, "I tried to reconcile with my husband one time, and he just will not reconcile." But have you tried seven times?

> "Do not give up!"
> Just because the door looks closed
> does not mean it will stay closed.

Some people say, "I received prayer for healing one time and nothing happened," so they gave up. They did not continue to put the Word of God in them and make the extra effort to go after what God has promised them. Other people trying to overcome an addiction will say, "I tried this and I tried that, and it did not work." But there comes a time when you have to resolve within yourself, "God opens doors that no man can shut, and the door God has for me is *going to open.*"

Our bear was to sell the auto mart building. In September 1984 we were making double monthly payments: $42,000 on the mortgage that we held on the auto mart site we had just vacated, and $30,000 on the facility we had just leased, for a total of $72,000 a month! We had been trying to sell the remodeled auto mart for over two years, but there was not one nibble on the line!

There were not a lot of churches in town that could envision themselves moving into a car dealership. It takes a revelation from God to see your church in mechanic bays that have been remodeled! We had a breezeway where you could punch a button and all the doors came up. We also had showroom windows—full glass from floor to ceiling—where we let the light of Jesus Christ shine out to those who were passing by during Sunday school and Victory Bible Institute classes held in that part of the building.

In November 1984, two months after moving into our leased facility, we received our one and only contact about buying the car dealership property. I learned that God can touch anyone He wants at anytime in anyplace. Sam Walton, the wealthiest man in America at that time, purchased our site for a Sam's Wholesale Club—and paid us $3.3 million just for the dirt! They removed the building and built new facilities for their store.

With the real estate closing in January 1985, we were completely out of debt! Whipping our bear took place over a process of time, but David did not just step on the scene and whip the giant in one day either. It started when he was about five years old with a little piece of leather and some rocks while he was working out in the fields. He built up to the moment where God could use him to guide the missile that was in his hand to the right spot on Goliath's head.

Our "giant" was to purchase land and build our own facilities on a cash basis. One day in 1982 while I was driving down South Lewis Avenue in Tulsa, in the Spirit I saw our facilities. I pulled over into the O.R.U. Mabee Center parking lot and sketched what I saw. I found out that Oral Roberts University owned the land. But when I talked with Brother Roberts, I discovered he was not interested in selling any land.

I wondered, "Did I miss it?" Yet, the vision had been so clear. Two years went by. During that time we did a land search all over town. I never shared my spiritual vision with the land search committee. At the end of their search, they unanimously said, "We believe we are supposed to be near O.R.U."

Then Brother Roberts asked us one day, "Where are you going to put your church?" I said, "We still feel we are supposed to be near O.R.U." Brother Roberts said, "I have been thinking about it lately. I do not feel I should sell you the land, but I would lease it to you." So in December 1984, he made us an offer to lease the land.

At that time, I had no peace about constructing a huge permanent building on leased land, so I just held onto the lease agreement until March of 1985. Then the Lord spoke to me while I was in prayer, "Sign the lease and I will work." After signing the lease, within one week we printed and distributed a brochure that announced our plans to build at 7700 South Lewis Avenue, across the street from O.R.U.'s Avenue of Flags.

Three weeks later, I received a call from Brother Roberts. Because of a challenge with the people managing the hotel nearby, which was built on land O.R.U. leased to them, Brother Roberts said to me, "We've got to get out of your lease."

The company who ran the hotel had violated their lease agreement and took a stand that legally and morally opposed O.R.U.'s standards. Brother Roberts said, "We cannot have a situation down the road where your church and the university would have a conflict. But I am a man of my word. Since you have already announced your plans to your people to build, the only thing I know to do is offer to sell you the land."

I did not cheer because, when we had done a land search, the cost of land around O.R.U. was extremely high! Brother Roberts said, "We will sell the land to you for $5 million cash, and you cannot borrow to buy it. You will have to come up with it now." That was kind of like saying, "You can vote if you can write in Chinese!" So I said, "Let me pray about it."

While I was in prayer, the Lord said, "Make an offer similar to the lease agreement." On the lease agreement, we were going to lease the front half of the land with a later option on the back half. God gave me two time frames, so I went back to Brother Roberts and made an offer to buy the front half of the land for $3.5 million, with an option on the back half at $1.5 million in a few years' time. I asked for seven months—from June 2, 1985, to January 2, 1986—to come up with the $3.5 million for the front land.

At that time, our budget for an entire year was not $3.5 million, so we would have to raise the $3.5 million on top of our entire normal budget—and do it in seven months. I said to Brother Roberts, "If it happens, it will be God, you will know it is God, I will know it is God, the people will know it is God, and God will know it is God!" Brother Roberts said, "Okay, it's a deal!"

At that time, we had about $700,000. Two weeks went by and we were not moving very fast toward the $3.5 million we needed. As I prayed, I asked, "Lord, what do we do?" He took me back to the story of David and Goliath. He said, "What did David do?"

I said, "He used what was in his hand."

The Lord asked me, "What is in your hand?"

I said, "What do You mean?"

He said, "What does your church have in its hand? How much money do you have?"

I responded, "We have $700,000." Then it hit me what God was implying. "You want us to give away the $700,000?"

The Lord said, "Yes."

In mid-June, 1985, I told our congregation. "The Lord has directed that we plant $700,000 into three areas—ministries that are meeting needs we are not meeting, into the poor, and into missions. We are going to give away $100,000 a month over the next seven months." As I shared this, it was like all the air went out of the Mabee Center where we were meeting!

We then proceeded to carry out this plan. When we came down to the last month before the $3.5 million was due, we were still $1 million away from our goal. I said, "Lord, we have done everything we can do."

The Lord spoke up inside of me and said, "No, you haven't done everything you can do." God gave us the idea to go on television live the very last night, Thursday, January 2, 1986. We went on at 6:00 p.m. and needed to raise approximately $300,000 that night to meet our midnight deadline. If we did not meet the deadline with the full $3.5 million, Brother Roberts was free from the obligation to sell us the land.

At 15 minutes till midnight, we were still slightly short of the money we needed. The agreement was that we would take the check to O.R.U.'s administrator at midnight. We had a blank check with us. Then at five minutes till midnight, we got in touch with our head accountant and asked, "Mike, do we have the money?" He said, "You can write the check!" Our giant was whipped! We delivered $3.5 million at the moment it was due. God was right on time! He was not early, but neither was He late.

We did not reach our goal by scoring a few home runs—big gifts that brought us quickly to $3.5 million. Instead, it was a succession of "base hits." It was steady progress. With every step around those bases we made time to know God, we understood our covenant with Him, we spoke and acted in faith, we used what we had as He led us, and we started small before tackling the bigger things.

God told us what we were to do. Our job was simply to obey and trust Him for the final outcome. He brought us across home plate again and again until it was done, and all the glory belongs to Him.

Now the same God who came through for us in our hour of need will come through for you. You just need to hang on to the winning strategy of the five principles I have just shared. They not only worked for David in the Bible, they have worked for us and countless others in similar difficult positions.

So take those five stones and start slinging!

Chapter 14

Heavenly Armor

NO BALLPLAYER, whether they are in Little League, American Legion, college, or the professional leagues, goes into a game without wearing special equipment to help them avoid injuries and play to win. Batting helmets, gloves, chest protectors, and special shoes are all part of a ballplayer's "armor." It helps them stand up to the rigors of the game. It protects them and enables them to meet the challenge of the opposition.

The spiritual armor of God is like that for us. It is protection against the devil who "...walks about like a roaring lion, seeking whom he may devour" (1 Pet. 5:8). When we put on the armor of God, we are better equipped to face the opposition, avoid injuries, and knock the curve balls out of the park. Paul described the armor in detail in chapter 6 of Ephesians:

> *Put on the whole armor of God, that you may be able to stand against the wiles of the devil. For we do not wrestle against flesh and blood, but against principalities, against powers, against the rulers of the darkness of this age, against spiritual hosts of wickedness in the heavenly places. Therefore take up the whole armor of God, that you may be able to withstand in the evil day, and having done all, to stand. Stand therefore, having girded your waist with truth, having put on*

the breastplate of righteousness, and having shod your feet with the preparation of the gospel of peace; above all, taking the shield of faith with which you will be able to quench all the fiery darts of the wicked one. And take the helmet of salvation, and the sword of the Spirit, which is the word of God; praying always with all prayer and supplication in the Spirit, being watchful to this end with all perseverance and supplication for all the saints.

(Ephesians 6:11-18)

Before Paul goes through each piece of the armor, he tells us that God's plan is for us to be able to stand against the wiles of the devil. God's plan is for success. God is a good God and the devil is a bad devil. And the devil has lots of wiles—lots of strategies to get you off track and away from the plans God has for your life.

When you are up at the plate, ready to bat, you can be sure the opposing team has strategies to get you to strike out. Sometimes, those strategies are all aimed right at you. But other times, they may be aimed at a teammate. In life, that may be your spouse, your children, or someone who is close to you. Instead of hurling the ball toward you, the pitcher may try to draw one of your teammates off first base and force an out. Let's look at the armor of God that will give you an advantage over your opponents.

Paul said, **"having put on the breastplate of righteousness."** If you are walking around in iniquity and unrighteousness, it is going to be pretty hard to fight the devil.

"Having girded your waist with truth...." If you are lying and deceiving someone—for example cheating on your income tax—and you start to resist the devil, there is going to be no way, Jose! And notice you are going to have to put on that belt of truth. It is an action you have to take yourself, not your pastor, your mom, or your spouse who prays every day for you.

"Having shod your feet with the preparation of the gospel of peace...." Are you doing all you can to proclaim the Good News? Are you on the advance—on the offensive—or have you got your shoes off, running in retreat? Paul says, "You are going to have to put on your 'go' shoes." Two-thirds of God's name spells GO. That is going with the gospel. The cleats on a ballplayer's shoes help him dig in as he is rounding the bases, running for home. Those cleats help him to stand and not lose his footing. The gospel is the same way. When we are going with the gospel, our footing will be sure.

"Taking the shield of faith...." A lot of people do not even know what a shield is. The shield of faith is your faith in God's Word. God said your faith will quench every fiery dart of the wicked one. He did not say that no fiery darts (curve balls) would be thrown at you. But He said that the shield of faith would stop every one of them.

But, as with the belt of truth, *you* are the one who has to put the shield of faith up there. You may feel like your shield is loaded down with fiery arrows, but thank God it is in place. Maybe you feel like diving for the dugout and launching for the locker room, but you can trust God's shield.

"Take the helmet of salvation...." You have to *know that you know that you know* that Jesus is your Lord and Savior. He is your Redeemer. Having done all to stand, you can know He is standing with you.

"And the sword of the Spirit...." We have already discussed the profession of our faith. Are you speaking the Word of God? Are you declaring God's Word? Is it a part of your life? God told Joshua, "You do not let that book of the law depart out of your mouth. You meditate in it day and night that you may observe to do it." (See Joshua 1:8.)

"Praying always with all prayer and supplication in the Spirit...." The last part of the armor Paul describes is prayer. He says we are to come to God *always*—and that means at all times, continually, every moment of the day. In other words, we are to have a lifestyle of prayer. We are to be *always* communicating with God.

When a player is up to bat, running the bases, or in the outfield, he is always looking to his coach for wisdom and direction. Christians are to have the same dependence upon God.

> When you step up to the plate in His armor, you have everything you need to succeed.

So suit up with the armor of God and always be in an attitude of prayer. And remember, your armor is *heavenly* armor. This is not something you pick up at a sporting goods store that falls apart after a few seasons' use. This armor is God's armor! And when you step up to the plate in His armor, you have everything you need to succeed.

Chapter 15

The Team Owner Is *for* You!

I F A PLAYER ON A TEAM is going through difficult times in practices or actual games, it can sure help if he knows the team owner likes him. The owner of a professional team can keep or trade a player. He can change a player to a position that suits him better or get him some special coaching. The team owner has influence over the players' salaries. Overall, it can make all the difference in the world if the team owner is for you.

In the same way, if you as a Christian *really* understand that God loves you and is for you, it can bring confidence, security, and peace—even if your performance has not been what it should be.

> *He chose us in Him before the foundation of the world, that we should be holy and without blame before Him in love.*
>
> (Ephesians 1:4)

> *Perfect love casts out fear.*
>
> (1 John 4:18)

Playing the game of life without fear—having confidence, security, and peace—can produce better performance. In

Romans 8, the apostle Paul wrote to the believers in the city of Rome. They were facing persecution, rejection, and obstacles. They were going through many difficulties. Nero was the Roman emperor, and one of Nero's greatest claims to fame was his persecution of Christians. Everyday life was filled with uncertainties.

Maybe you are also facing persecution, rejection, and obstacles. Or maybe someone you know and care about is going through many difficulties and uncertainties. The letter Paul wrote to the Romans is just as relevant for you and me today. I am going to share some things from verses 28 through 39 that I believe will help you and encourage you. In verse 28, Paul writes:

> *And we know that all things work together for good to those who love God, to those who are the called according to His purpose.*

As you are reading this, stop a moment and say these words out loud: "All things work together for good." Now look at the two conditions in the second half of the verse. The promise that all things work together for good is first of all *"to those who love God."* How do you know that you love God? According to the Bible, those who love God keep His commandments. First John 5:3 says, "For this is the love of God, that we keep His commandments. And His commandments are not burdensome."

If you say that you love someone, but you never do what they ask you to do, you are really talking out of both sides of your mouth!

Those who keep God's commandments are those who love Him. And to them, obeying God is not a weight or a burden. You know, if you say that you love someone, but you never do what they ask you to do, you are really talking out of both sides of your mouth!

At different times, we are all faced with evaluating the character of people. It could be a job opportunity, a church activity, or something at school. As we pray for God's guidance on the choices that come our way, we can look at the folks involved. You can usually perceive that certain people love God by this very practical, simple, and easy test: People who love God are obeying His commandments. There are a lot of people who say they love God, but all you have to do is look at their life. The proof is in their actions.

The second condition of God's promise is "...*to those who are the called according to His purpose.*" What does that mean? It means that all things work together for good for those people who have surrendered their will and said, "Lord, Your will be done, not mine. I have accepted Your calling and I want Your purpose in my life."

You see, for self-willed, independent people who are demanding their own way, things are not going to work together for good. Why? Because even if God sent a blessing their way, they would never meet up with it. The blessing of God would be coming their way, but they would take another turn, go their own way, and do something else. They would be frustrating the plans and purposes of God for their lives.

But for those who are called according to God's purposes, when God sends blessings—they meet those blessings head-on! Their lives intersect with God's blessing because they already submitted themselves to follow the path that God has for them. Hallelujah!

Do you love God? Have you accepted God's calling for His purpose in your life? Then get ready, because all things are working together for good.

For whom he foreknew, He also predestined to be conformed to the image of His Son, that He might be the firstborn among many brethren.

(Romans 8:29)

> We may go to different places,
> follow different career tracks,
> have different family situations,
> and so forth, but the bottom line
> for every one of us—our goal and
> our purpose—is to be like Jesus.

Jesus Christ, God's Son, is the model. He is the pattern. God planned that everyone who would believe in Jesus Christ would be conformed to His image. Or to say it another way, God planned for you to be like Jesus. Your purpose in this life is to be like Him. Now, we may go to different places, follow different career tracks, have different family situations, and so forth, but the bottom line for every one of us—our goal and our purpose—is to be like Jesus, that we might be conformed to His image.

Moreover whom He predestined, these He also called; whom He called, He also justified; and whom He justified, these He also glorified.

(Romans 8:30)

This simply says that God has plans for those who accept His Son. And every one who has accepted Him has responded to that call. Many people have heard the call of God to be saved and they have responded. And those He has called, He has justified, meaning He has declared them not guilty. When God justifies us, we are acquitted for the things we have done wrong. We are declared innocent because of the blood of His Son, Jesus. That is why we can rest assured that the "owner of the team" likes us!

Then, once He declares us innocent or justified, He glorifies us. That means He puts His life in us. He puts His nature in us. He puts His Spirit in us. To have the glory of God is to have the life of God. And the more we let that life shine out of us, the more others can see God's glory coming from us. People are drawn to the glory of God's joy, His peace, and His love radiating out from us. When God glorifies us, He is simply showing Himself through our lives. Acts 17:28 says, "for in Him we live and move and have our being...For we are also His offspring." Say it: "I have been called, justified, and glorified."

What then shall we say to these things? If God is for us, who can be against us?

(Romans 8:31)

If the owner of the team is *for* you, then what is happening with the other players or fans is not that important! Paul is evidently addressing some things that were happening in the lives of those believers in Rome. He was telling them, "What are you going to say in light of all these circumstances you are going through?" He was asking them to look at what was happening in the world in light of what God had spoken.

People are drawn to the glory of God's joy, His peace, and His love radiating out from us.

The same is true for you today. In light of what God has done, what difference do your circumstances make? *Who* can be against you? If God votes for you, you win! It only takes one vote—His. If God votes for you and pulls the lever on your behalf, then whatever rises up against you is going to experience the bad end of the deal.

If God votes for you, you win!

If individuals or situations try to oppose you, then they come up against God. Why? Because God called you, justified you, and glorified you. He is now living in you, so an attack against you is an attack against Him. Hallelujah! Who can be against you?

Many people—even Spirit-filled believers—live in fear of a circumstance, a person, or even a group of people being against them. They read or hear about something happening to someone else and they begin thinking the same thing will happen to them. I am praying for a Holy Ghost explosion in your mind that you will quit saying, "I wonder what is going to happen?" Instead, you will start saying, "Oh, glory to God, all things are working together for good because God is for me. Who can be against me?"

> *He who did not spare His own Son, but delivered Him up for us all, how shall He not with Him also freely give us all things?*
>
> (Romans 8:32)

God loved the world so much, He gave His only Son, Jesus Christ. Jesus gave His blood—suffering a terrible death on the cross in our place. He was buried, but on the third day He was raised from the dead. Paul is saying, "If God did not stop short from giving us His best, Jesus, would He not also freely give us anything and everything of lesser value?" Think of it. If God would give the best that He has, why would He withhold anything else?

We need to change our thinking. Instead of focusing on all the things we need, we should start thanking God that He has promised to give us everything we need in Jesus Christ. He will give us everything to meet the practical needs in our lives as we trust in Him.

You may be needing a mate or money or healing or peace. As you pray in the name of Jesus, God can, will, and does provide the things that are needed in this life. You see, He is a very practical God. He made and designed us, spirit, soul, and body. He knows exactly what we need and He has already made provision for everything human beings require. But He asks that we put Him first and seek His Kingdom first. Then He says, "All these things will be added to you."

> *Who shall bring a charge against God's elect? It is God who justifies. Who is he who condemns? It is Christ who died, and furthermore is also risen, who is even at the right hand of God, who also makes intercession for us.*
>
> (Romans 8:33-34)

Condemnation points at your sin and then points to the punishment. Conviction points at your sin and then points to the cross.

Jesus Christ is praying for us right now. So Paul asks, "Who can condemn us? Who can put us down or bring a charge against us?" God has said, "Not guilty." Through the death of Jesus Christ, we have been declared forgiven. Remember this: God does not condemn you. His Holy Spirit will convict you to repent, but it is the devil who condemns.

Condemnation points at your sin and then points to the punishment. Conviction points at your sin and then points to the cross. Jesus paid the price so we could receive forgiveness and mercy. If Jesus did that for you and me, then who can condemn us? Who can judge us? God has already passed the sentence. The judgment has already fallen on His Son. We have been declared not guilty. Lift up your head today—your condemnation and guilt have been removed!

> *Who shall separate us from the love of Christ? Shall tribulation, or distress, or persecution, or famine, or nakedness, or peril, or sword?*
>
> (Romans 8:35)

Tribulation means troubles or hard times. Are you having a little stress? Are you being persecuted for your faith in Christ?

> *As it is written: "For your sake we are killed all the day long; we are accounted as sheep for the slaughter." Yet in all these things we are more than conquerors through Him who loved us.*
>
> (Romans 8:36-37)

His is not a distant, indifferent, passive love; it is an active, motivated, progressive love that is coming right toward you.

Do not think lowly of yourself or your circumstances in the game of life, because God owns the universe, and *He likes you!* In fact, He loves you and will help you in every area of your life.

In spite of the difficulty, in spite of the opposition, in spite of the problems, Paul says we are more than conquerors. He is not saying we are going to be, hoping to be, or praying it comes to pass. He says, we are. So if we are, then I am. Say it out loud, "If we are, then I am more than a conqueror."

> *For I am persuaded that neither death nor life, nor angels, nor principalities nor powers, nor things present nor things to come, nor height nor depth, nor any other created thing, shall be able to separate us from the love of God which is in Christ Jesus our Lord.*

> (Romans 8:38-39)

"For I am persuaded...." Are you persuaded of these things? Or do you just think it sounds like a good idea? Do you just think it sounds like a good philosophy or good theology? Paul says, "I am persuaded." You see, all of these things can be true, but they will not affect your life until you are persuaded of them.

It does not matter what the devil or the world throws at us or what the flesh tries to do. Nothing can separate us from the love of God. So what is the bottom line? If God loves you and you cannot be separated from that love, then you have His help. His is not a distant, indifferent, passive love; it is an active, motivated, progressive love that is coming right toward you. You cannot be separated from God by the things the devil will bring through his principalities, powers, and works of darkness.

Do not think lowly of yourself or your circumstances in the game of life, because God owns the universe, and *He likes you!* In fact, He loves you and will help you in every area of your life. He can help you pitch, catch, run—and even hit the curve balls in life like you never dreamed.

Remember, the Owner of the team is *for* you!

Chapter 16

Be an All-Star for the Kingdom of God

EVERY YEAR IN JULY, baseball players from the American and National Leagues play in the All-Star Game. It is considered the halfway point in the baseball season and it is a time the fans can watch the most popular and talented players in the sport all play at the same time. How well a player has been playing at that point in the season (and in his career) has a lot to do with whether or not he is selected for the All-Star Team. In one game, you can watch all the best players in professional baseball at every position: pitcher, shortstop, outfielder, and all the others.

When Orel Hershiser was named to the All-Star team in 1988—the same year he won the National League's Cy Young award—he did not play third base and he did not play shortstop. Hershiser is a pitcher. He is a very talented pitcher who loves the Lord. When he is out on the ball field, he sticks to pitching because that is his talent; that is his gift. God has put talents and gifts in all of us. Our job is to know our calling and to walk in it.

A Christian man named J.C. Penney founded a chain of very successful department stores. Mr. Penney loved the Lord and he ran his company with godly leadership, giving much of his corporate and personal wealth to the church.

> Every person has unique gifts and talents from the Lord. When we discover those talents and use them for God's glory, then we are All-Stars on His team.

R.G. LeTourneau was an inventor of heavy machinery. God gave him designs for massive earth-moving equipment that are used in mining. He even received the design for a special part of a machine in a dream and got up in the middle of the night to draw what he'd seen. Toward the end of his life, he was giving 90 percent of his income to the Lord and living on the other 10 percent.

My point is this: Every person has unique gifts and talents from the Lord. When we discover those talents and use them for God's glory, then we are All-Stars on His team—we are functioning in the place where we can achieve the most good for the Kingdom of God.

God did not give me the talent to design industrial machinery. But if that had been His will for me and I gave my best effort for Him in that field, the outcome would bring Him honor. Sharon shops in department stores, but she was not called to run one. She was called as a psalmist and worship leader, among other things. That is her talent and gift—and when she uses it for God, there are great results. People even get healed just listening to her sing.

What is God's call on your life? There are many, many outstanding servants of God who are not called into full-time ministry, but whose lives are dramatically affecting the Kingdom of God. There are Christian educators in our public schools; Christian doctors, nurses, and dentists; Christian truck drivers, retail clerks, airline pilots, and scientists.

Using your talents for the Lord in your sphere of influence, you can minister constantly and have opportunity after opportunity to lead people to Christ. That was the example Jesus gave us. He did not spend all His time in church. He was in the streets, the fields, the marketplaces—where the lost were living their daily lives.

Every believer has a role to play in the Kingdom of God. In Second Corinthians 12, Paul compares a human body to the Body of Christ. He talks about every part of the human body being important to the whole, just the same as it is in the Body of Christ:

> If the foot should say, "Because I am not a hand, I am not of the body," is it therefore not of the body? And if the ear should say, "Because I am not an eye, I am not of the body," is it therefore not of the body? If the whole body were an eye, where would be the hearing? If the whole were hearing, where would be the smelling? But now God has set the members, each one of them, in the body just as He pleased. And if they were all one member, where would the body be? But now indeed there are many members, yet one body. And the eye cannot say to the hand, "I have no need of you," nor again the head to the feet, "I have no need of you."

> (1 Corinthians 12:15-21)

There are no "spare parts" in the Body of Christ! Many people have accepted the gospel, but as far as Kingdom business is concerned, they have been idle. It is not that they are unconcerned or do not care, but they never really sensed an enlistment from God.

Maybe you are saying, "I am not sure I have been called. I have not sensed that I am one to be used in the service of the Lord." I want to help you see that God has a place for each of us. It is a place of labor for His Kingdom to help bring in the harvest in these last days.

Evangelist T.L. Osborn tells the story that when he was growing up on his family's farm, when harvesttime came there were not enough workers to gather all the harvest. There is a short time frame for the harvest, and it can be lost if it is not brought in during that time frame. Near Tulsa, in Bixby, there are migrant workers who come during the harvest of summer vegetable crops. Those migrant workers are needed because the farmers do not have enough hands with their regular workers.

Every year, migrant workers follow the wheat harvest from Oklahoma and Kansas up through Nebraska and on toward Canada. The natural harvest of crops is a picture of what is going on in the Kingdom of God. We are in harvesttime and God is enlisting workers.

You do not have to stand in the pulpit, be on the mission field, or be drawing your salary from a church to be one of God's workers in the harvest. God will make sure you are paid; He will provide your way. I want to broaden your view of the ministry and help you see there is a place for every person in the Body of Christ.

God did not make any parts of His Body that did not have a function—work to do, a job to do. You have a part to play in the harvest, whether it is reaping it, storing it, conserving it, preserving it, or many other things. That is a picture of the ministry we have to people.

> There is a place for every person
> in the Body of Christ.

The Bible says many are called, but few are chosen. (See Matthew 20:16.) There have been lots of interpretations of that

Scripture, but most theologians would agree that there are many people who hear the call of God, but they do not choose to prepare themselves and receive that calling. Just like on any level of athletic play, there is preparation. There is learning, practice, physical conditioning, and team meetings. Those things happen before you play a real game, and they happen before you step into your calling.

> God is looking for people who will take on the work that needs to be done because it needs to be done— not for any recognition they may get.

I thank God for the faithful people who teach Sunday school, who work with our youth, our musicians, and choir members, and on and on. These positions are callings of God. These people have practiced and prepared to work in these different areas of our church. Mark 10:43-45 says that if you want to be great in the Kingdom of God, you have to be willing to be the servant of all. God is looking for people who will take on the work that needs to be done because it needs to be done—not for any recognition they may get.

How did Sharon and I get started? No one was paying us; that never really crossed our minds. We got saved and began teaching Sunday school. We started working with young people. Whether or not you ever get paid for it, you can be a minister—a servant of the Lord Jesus Christ. You can take a role Long before many of our pastoral assistants were ever on staff, they were serving and filling a need in the church.

When we came to O.R.U., our background was United Methodist. So Sharon and I went to a Methodist church and we searched out people and said, "Can we do something?" We wanted to do something for God. I worked with a high school Sunday school class and Sharon taught the 4- and 5-year-olds.

When you want to do something and you cannot just sit there, then you have the call of God on your life. It could be any number of areas, and it does not mean you cannot work a regular, secular job somewhere. For us, we worked to pay for school and our living expenses, but we also wanted to be doing something for the Kingdom of God. And here is the reason: Whatever you do for the Kingdom of God will last into eternity.

We saw that working at our jobs would help us eat and get through school, but it was not going to count for anything in eternity. We wanted to be doing something that would last past the grave. There is a time to come when we will give account to God, and then we will enjoy spending eternity in a great relationship with Him. But our rewards will be related to what we do right here on this earth.

Perhaps you sense you have a call of God on your life. You may be wondering, "How do I confirm it? How do I know His call for sure?" When I had just turned 16 and had a job as a janitor at a radio station, I wanted to make some more money. So I tested whether I was called to work at a particular pizza place. Because I played sports all year long and had practices after school, the time I could work was after that. The job at the pizza place was the late night shift, cleaning up from midnight to 2 A.M. It only took me one night to get a revelation that I was not called to work that shift! People laugh when I tell that story, but that job just did not fit. So I went back to what I had been doing before.

When you step in and begin to serve in an area, you will find out whether you fit or not. And it may take two or three different jobs until you find the one that is suited to you. One woman in our church asked about working in a particular area. She tried it and it just did not fit. Then she tried another area and that did not fit either. Finally she found a place in administration, helping undergird the work in our missions school. Her background was as an executive secretary, and eventually she was hired to help facilitate that area of the ministry. She found the place where she fit by simply volunteering.

There is a place where every one of us fits. It may take a little experimentation, seeking the Lord, and volunteering in different areas. But God says that those who are faithful in a few things will become rulers over many things. (See Matthew 25:14-30.) This is how you get into the ministry. Find where you fit, become faithful there, and you will become fruitful. Faithful first, and then fruitful as a result.

> ## Find where you fit, become faithful there, and you will become fruitful.

In the Kingdom of God, you can be a little producer, a large producer, or a great producer. Jesus talked about this in the parable of the talents. It is a picture of the way things work in the Kingdom of God. When we are faithful with whatever He entrusts to us, whether it is money, ability, or the gifts of the Spirit, we can become reproducers in the Kingdom of God.

If you are diligent and you study and develop yourself, God will use you. Sometimes people despise education, training, and preparation time, but it is really hard for God to bless laziness and ignorance. It is your choice, and I challenge you to decide right now, "I am going to accept the call of God on my life." Make yourself available to God and determine that you are going to try different opportunities until you find the one that fits you.

When you go after that call of God, you will do whatever it takes to seek it out and search it out and find your place in the Body of Christ. When you ask God to use you, you had better mean it, because He will. There will be demands on your life because you are His servant. But when you are playing the position God pre-ordained for your life—with the unique talents and abilities He put in you—you will be doing things that will last into eternity.

People will see your good works and glorify the Father. (See Matthew 5:16.) God's "team" will be better off because you have utilized your talents for Him.

Chapter 17

Going From
Player to Coach

WHEN YOU BEGIN TO REALLY LIVE your life by the Word of God,
you will probably discover two things. The victories you
begin to experience will be noticed by the people around you,
and you will become eager to share with others what you have
learned.

After I had been saved several months, the Lord spoke to
me, saying, "What have you ever done for others?" I began to
reflect on the fact that everything I did was basically selfish. My
work studies, sports activities, and friendships were all for me.

At that point I began to think about what I could do for God
and for others. It occurred to me that I could coach a Boys'
Club basketball team. Naturally, I started sharing Christ with
those 9- and 10-year-olds each week at the practices. It was my
work with those boys that caused the director of the Club to
ask me to direct the summer sports and camp programs, and
that experience prepared me for many ministry opportunities
that followed.

God did not save you to sit in the dugout and watch the
game. Nor did He just want you playing the game. No, as you're
learning to play by His rules and to give it all you've got, He
wants you to encourage others and teach them what you have
learned. We have a never-ending debt of love to other people.

When Jesus was sending His disciples out to spread the gospel, Matthew 10:8 says He told them, "Freely you have received, freely give."

> ## We have a never-ending debt of love to other people.

The apostle Paul was like a father and coach to his spiritual son, Timothy. In Second Timothy 2:2, he wrote:

And the things that you have heard from me among many witnesses, commit these to faithful men who will be able to teach others also.

Each person who receives God's love is supposed to give it out. That is God's plan. When you begin to coach and encourage others, your own skills will continue to mature and grow. In fact, you can only receive in accordance to what you give.

Sometimes it is the encouragement and coaching of others that puts us over the top. It is what drives us to go beyond what we think we are capable of. When I was a teenager, I loved sports of all kinds, and one of them was track. In many track events, people are running for speed, as opposed to distance. Every second counts and you push yourself to the limits of your ability.

In junior high school I ran in a one-lap, 440-yard race. When it came my turn to run, I was giving it all I had, concentrating on the finish line. All of a sudden—off to the side—I heard this voice calling out, "Come on, Billy Joe. Come on, Billy Joe!" I was not wanting to lose my concentration, but I looked over and saw my dad. He was so excited—wanting me to do well—that he had come down on the infield of the track and was running beside me! He was calling out encouragement to me and urging me on to the finish line, shouting, "Come on, Billy Joe!"

As I pictured that memory in my mind one day, I realized that it was a picture of what Jesus is doing in our lives. He is so excited about the plans He has for us. He wants us to do well, to excel, and to have the victory over every obstacle. He is beside us, running with us, day in and day out. He is saying, "Come on, you can do it. If I am for you, who can be against you? I love you. I care about you. I want you to have the victories I have planned for your life."

Sometimes you need to be there *for someone else*, like my dad was there for me that day. You need to see their potential, like a father sees his son's potential. You need to get involved—so involved that you stop thinking about your own needs or what is on *your* agenda—and take a few minutes or hours to give yourself wholeheartedly to encourage someone else in *their* race.

> You can only receive
> in accordance to what you give.

The writer of Hebrews makes it very plain that we have an obligation to teach others. He was not talking to the pastors or the church leaders; he was talking to all believers. The Living Bible puts it this way:

> *You have been Christians a long time now, and you ought to be teaching others, but instead you have dropped back to the place where you need someone to teach you all over again the very first principles in God's Word. You are like babies who can drink only milk, not old enough for solid food. And when a person is still living on milk it shows he is not very far along in the Christian life, and does not know much about the difference between right and wrong. He is still a baby-Christian! You will never be able to eat solid spiritual*

*food and understand the deeper things of God's Word
until you become better Christians and learn right from
wrong by practicing doing right.*

(Hebrews 5:12-14 TLB)

Did you catch that last phrase, "practicing doing right"? God is not looking for perfection. He just wants you to be out there practicing and doing the best you can. We are to be witnessing and sharing the gospel with other people all the time. Our job is to get up to the plate and witness. The result is in the hands of the Holy Spirit. He is the One who makes the heart of the lost person ready to receive the Good News you are delivering. If the person does not want to hear what you have to say, they have not rejected you, they have rejected God.

You need to get involved—so involved that you stop thinking about your own needs or what is on *your* agenda—and take a few minutes or hours to give yourself wholeheartedly to encourage someone else in *their* race.

Then many will *not* reject God and they will be saved and set free! Now you have got a "rookie Christian" on your hands. It is up to you as *coach* to encourage that person and see that he or she gets plugged into a church where they can be nurtured and get a solid foundation of the Word of God.

We need to be coaching others in their Christian walk, because it is the natural result of growing up spiritually and the love of God is in our hearts for others. The Bible says that Jesus did not come to do away with the Law, but to fulfill it. What that means is that the only way we can even attempt to fulfill the Law is to have Jesus in our hearts. It is His character of love living inside our own hearts that makes it possible for us not to kill, steal, covet, or violate any of the other commandments. His nature, imparted to us when we are born again, is the only way to succeed in these areas.

> The only way we can even attempt to fulfill the Law is to have Jesus in our hearts.

The new believer's need for people to coach, teach, and encourage them is desperate. God is counting on you and me. He does not have an alternative plan. Jesus gave the commission of evangelism and discipleship to people. It is up to us to fulfill His plan.

Teaching others makes us dig deeper into the Word of God and prayer. All children go through a phase when they seem to be constantly asking, "Why?" They have a natural curiosity about everything they see and experience. They are not looking for an encyclopedia-type answer; they just need a simple, honest response, even if it is, "I do not know." New Christians are just like kids sometimes. Every time they open the Bible, they learn something new and they have lots of questions. We will add to our own growth as we help answer their questions.

The Great Commission says that we are not only to preach the gospel to all nations, but also to make disciples of them. Jesus said, "Teaching them to observe all things that I have commanded you" (Matt. 28:20).

God is not looking for perfection. He just wants you to be out there practicing and doing the best you can.

If you ask God, He will give you "Timothys" in your life to coach and encourage. Likewise, you need to be accountable to a Paul, someone from whom you are still learning and receiving coaching and encouragement. Remember, we are not in a nine-inning game! God has given us His Word, the power of prayer, heavenly armor, winning strategies from the Holy Spirit, and a blood covenant with His Son, Jesus Christ. Stand up to the plate, feet firmly planted on the Rock who holds through every storm, eyes fixed on the Author and Finisher of your faith, knowing with certainty that:

He who dwells in the secret place of the Most High shall remain stable and fixed under the shadow of the Almighty (Whose power no foe can withstand).

(Psalm 91:1 AMP)

Now go knock 'em out of the park!

Teaching others makes us dig deeper into the Word of God and prayer.

Appendix

100 Scriptural Meditations for Hitting the Curve Balls in Life

HERE ARE 100 SAMPLE CONFESSIONS randomly selected and created from God's Word, personalized just for you! As you begin to make these confessions a part of your daily meditation time with the Lord, you will soon find yourself standing at the "batter's plate," facing life with the peace, confidence, and assurance that can only come from God.

Speak these confessions *aloud*. As you do, you will be strengthened in your spirit, able to "keep your eye on the ball, adjust your timing, and turn your curve balls into home runs!"

1. I am diligent to present myself approved of God, unashamed, rightly dividing the word of truth—His Word! (See Second Timothy 2:15.)

2. I am seated in heavenly places in Christ Jesus. (See Ephesians 2:6.)

3. I am God's workmanship, created in Christ Jesus for good works, which God prepared for me to walk in. (See Ephesians 2:10.)

4. God's Word will not depart from my mouth, but I will meditate in it day and night, that I may observe to do according to all that is written in it. Then my way will be prosperous, and I will have good success. (See Joshua 1:8.)

5. Because I diligently obey the voice of the Lord my God and observe carefully all of His commandments, God will set me high above all nations of the earth. I am blessed in the city and in the country; in the fruit of my body; (in the work to which He has called me; and in my checking and savings accounts). I am blessed when I come in and blessed when I go out. The Lord causes my enemies who rise against me to be defeated before my face. Though they come against me one way, they will flee from me seven ways. The Lord commands His blessings on everything to which I set my hand and blesses the land that He has given me. The Lord has established me as holy to Himself and has abundantly blessed and increased me with His good treasure. I will lend and not borrow. The Lord has made me the head and not the tail, above and not beneath. I will not turn away from any of God's commands. Instead, I accept the full counsel of His Word, in Jesus' name. (See Deuteronomy 28:1-14.)

6. In Christ, I have been redeemed from the curse of the law. Abraham's blessings are mine now, in this life. (See Galatians 3:13-14.)

7. God is increasing me more and more. (See Psalm 115:14.)

8. I shall not die but live, and declare the works of the Lord. (See Psalm 118:17.)

9. Because the Lord is my Shepherd, I shall not want. (See Psalm 23:1.)

10. Goodness and mercy will follow me all the days of my life. (See Psalm 23:6.)

11. The Spirit of the Lord is upon me to share the Good News of Jesus Christ with others; to heal the broken-hearted; to proclaim liberty to the captives and sight to the blind; and to set at liberty those who are oppressed. (See Luke 4:18.)

12. In Christ and in God's Word, He has given me all things that pertain to life and godliness. (See Second Peter 1:3.)

13. As I sing and praise the Lord, He sets ambushments against my enemies. (See Second Chronicles 20:22.)

14. The blessing of the Lord makes me rich, and He adds no sorrow with it. (See Proverbs 10:22.)

15. God has not given me a spirit of fear, but of power and of love and of a sound mind. (See Second Timothy 1:7.)

16. God's thoughts of me are of peace and not of evil. His plans for me are to prosper me and not to harm me, to give me hope and a future. (See Jeremiah 29:11 NIV.)

17. I am not slothful, but I imitate those who through faith and patience inherit the promises of God. (See Hebrews 6:12.)

18. The peace of God guards my heart and mind through Christ Jesus. (See Philippians 4:7.)

19. In Jesus' name, I cast down imaginations and every high thing that exalts itself against the knowledge of God, bringing every thought into captivity to the obedience of Christ and His Word. I think on those things which are true, noble, just, pure, lovely and of good report. (See Second Corinthians 10:5; Philippians 4:8.)

20. I am born again through Jesus Christ, and I am baptized in the Spirit of God to be a witness of Him in the earth. His ability and enablement are mine for the work to which He has called me. (See John 3:16; Acts 1:8.)

21. Because I am willing and obedient, I am eating the good of the land. (See Isaiah 1:19.)

22. God gives me the power to get wealth and teaches me to profit. He also leads me in the way I should go. (See Deuteronomy 8:18; Isaiah 48:17.)

23. God's plan for me is that I would prosper and be in health, just as my soul prospers. My soul is prospering (mind, will and emotions) with daily doses of God's Word! (See Third John 1:2.)

24. God takes pleasure in my prosperity. (See Psalm 35:27.)

25. My steps are ordered of the Lord, and He delights Himself in me. (See Psalm 37:23.)

26. Because I seek first the Kingdom of God and His righteousness, everything I need is added unto me. (See Matthew 6:33.)

27. Greater is He who is in me than he who is in the world. (See First John 4:4.)

28. Because I abide in the Lord and He abides in me—in His Word, in prayer and in communion—I bear good fruit: love, joy, peace, longsuffering, kindness, goodness, faithfulness, gentleness and self-control. (See John 15:5; Galatians 5:22-23.)

29. I cast all of my cares—anxieties, worries, and concerns—once and for all on the Lord, for He cares for me affectionately and cares about me watchfully. (See Second Peter 5:7 AMP.)

30. I hold fast the confession of God's Word without wavering, for He is faithful. He is not a man that He should lie or that He should repent, but He will do exactly as He has spoken. (See Hebrews 10:23; Numbers 23:19.)

31. I will not be afraid, but I will stand still and see the salvation (the delivering, saving, healing, restoring and preservation power) of the Lord. The enemy I see today I will see no more. The Lord will fight for me, and I will hold my peace. (See Exodus 14:13-14.)

32. The eyes of the Lord run to and fro throughout the whole earth, to show Himself strong in my behalf because my heart is loyal to Him. (See Second Chronicles 16:9.)

33. As I humble myself before my heavenly Father, pray, seek His face and turn from my wicked ways, I will hear from Heaven, He will forgive my sin and heal my land (my marriage and family, job, business, relationships, emotions, spirit, mind, finances, ministry and every area that concerns me). (See Second Chronicles 7:14.)

34. The joy of the Lord is my strength. (See Nehemiah 8:10.)

35. A merry heart does good like medicine. I have made a decision to let joy, laughter, and rejoicing be a vital part of my personality. (See Proverbs 17:22; Philippians 4:4.)

36. My gift makes room for me and brings me before great men. (See Proverbs 18:16.)

37. Lord Jesus, You are my healer. Because I serve You willfully and joyfully, You bless my bread and water and take sickness away from my midst. I will not suffer miscarriage or be barren in the land You have given me. In You, Lord Jesus, I will fulfill the number of my days. (See Exodus 15:26; 23:25-26.)

38. Thank You, Lord Jesus, for bearing sin, sickness and infirmities and poverty for me. By the stripes and wounds You took at Calvary, I am healed. (See Matthew 8:17; First Peter 2:24; Isaiah 53:5.)

39. Thank You, Lord, for restoring to me the years the locusts have eaten. I will eat in plenty and be satisfied and praise Your name, Lord, because You have dealt wondrously with me. (See Joel 2:25-26.)

40. The natural and/or spiritual children You have given me, Lord, are for signs and wonders, causing great glory to come to Your Kingdom, in Jesus' name. They will be strong in You and carry out great exploits! (See Isaiah 8:18; Daniel 11:32.)

41. Because I sow bountifully, I reap bountifully. I am a cheerful giver. Because of Your grace, Lord, I have all sufficiency in all things and Your abundance for every good work. (See Second Corinthians 9:6-8.)

42. My promotions do not come from the east, the west, or the south. They come from the Lord. (See Psalm 75:6-7.)

43. My body is the temple of the Holy Spirit who is in me. He bought me at a great price. Therefore, I will glorify God in my body, mind, and spirit, which are His. (See First Corinthians 6:19-20.)

44. I am accepted in the Beloved. (See Ephesians 1:6.)

45. I am seated with Christ in heavenly places. (See Ephesians 2:6.)

46. Because I obey my parents in the Lord and honor them, it will be well with me and I will live long on the earth. (See Ephesians 6:1-3.)

47. God is doing exceedingly abundantly above all that I ask or think, according to His power that is at work in me. His power in me increases daily because of my intake and meditation upon His Word. (See Ephesians 3:20.)

48. No corrupt communication will proceed out of my mouth, but only words that are good for edification, to impart God's grace to the hearers. I will not grieve the Holy Spirit with wrong thoughts and attitudes, in Jesus' name. (See Ephesians 5:29-30.)

49. I am kind to others, tenderhearted and forgiving, even as God in Christ forgives me. (See Ephesians 4:32.)

50. I put on the whole armor of God, so I can stand against the tricks and deceit of the devil: the belt of truth; the breastplate of righteousness; the preparation of the gospel of peace on my feet; the shield of faith to quench every fiery dart of the wicked one; the helmet of salvation; the sword of the Spirit, which is the Word of God; and all prayer and supplication in my understanding and in the Spirit. (See Ephesians 6:10-18.)

51. Integrity and uprightness preserve me. (See Psalm 25:21.)

52. Because I am like a sheep in the midst of wolves, I am wary and wise as a serpent, innocent, harmless, guileless, and without falsity as a dove. (See Matthew 10:16 AMP.)

53. Whatever my hand finds to do for the good of God's Kingdom, I do it with all my might. (See Ecclesiastes 9:10.)

54. No weapon formed against me shall prosper. Every tongue that speaks against me will be silenced. (See Isaiah 54:17.)

55. I release former failures and reliance on successes so God can do a new thing in my life. He will make roads in the wilderness and rivers in the desert for me, in Jesus' name. (See Isaiah 43:18-19.)

56. I will not be afraid or dismayed, for God is with me. He is my God, and He is for me. He will strengthen me, help me and uphold me with His victorious right hand of rightness and justice. God is for me, so who can withstand me? (See Isaiah 41:10 AMP; Romans 8:31.)

57. I will not grow weary in doing good, for in due season I will reap, because I will not faint or lose heart. (See Galatians 6:9.)

58. God always causes me to triumph in Christ, as a trophy of His victory. Through me He spreads and makes evident the fragrance of the knowledge of God. (See Second Corinthians 2:14 AMP.)

59. I am longsuffering and kind. I will not envy, parade myself or become puffed up in arrogance and pride. I will not behave rudely, seek things for my own benefit, become provoked or think evil. I will rejoice in the truth rather than in iniquity. I will bear all things, believe all things, hope all things, and endure all things. God's love in and through me never fails. (See First Corinthians 13:4-8.)

60. The Lord will deliver me out of *every* affliction and trouble. He will guard my bones so not one of them is broken. (See Psalm 34:17,19-20.)

61. As I wait upon the Lord, my strength is renewed. I mount up with wings like an eagle, I run and do not become weary and I walk and do not faint. (See Isaiah 40:31.)

62. I will bless the Lord at all times, for He forgives all of my sins, heals all of my diseases, redeems my life from destruction, crowns me with lovingkindness and good things, and renews my youth like an eagle. (See Psalm 103:3-5.)

63. I am not afraid of evil tidings, for my heart is steadfast, trusting in the Lord. (See Psalm 112:7.)

64. The stability of my life is the wisdom and knowledge of God. (See Isaiah 33:6.)

65. God will supply all of my needs according to His riches in glory by Christ Jesus. (See Philippians 4:19.)

66. I forget those things which are behind and reach forward to those things which are ahead. I press toward the goal for the prize of the upward call of God in Christ Jesus. (See Philippians 3:13-14.)

67. God's Word is a lamp to my feet and a light to my path. (See Psalm 119:105.)

68. In Christ, I can run through a troop and leap over a wall. (See Psalm 18:29.)

69. God is my refuge and fortress, in Him I will trust. He will deliver me from the snare of the devil. He will cover me with His feathers, and under His wings I will take refuge. His truth (His Word) is my shield and buckler. I will not be afraid of the terror by night, nor of the arrow that flies by day, nor of the pestilence that walks in darkness, nor of the destruction that lays waste at noonday. Although a thousand may fall at my side and ten thousand at my right hand, it shall not come near me. Because the Lord is my refuge and dwelling place, no evil will befall me, nor any plague come near my dwelling. God has given His angels charge over me to keep me in all my ways. I will trample the works of the devil underfoot. Because my focus and love are set upon the Lord, He will deliver me, set me on high and answer me. He will be with me in trouble, He will honor me and satisfy me with long life. He will show me His salvation, which includes healing, deliverance, preservation, and safety. (See Psalm 91.)

70. I am flourishing like a palm tree and growing like a cedar in Lebanon. Because I am planted in the house of the Lord, I am flourishing in the courts of my God. (See Psalm 92:12-13.)

71. Everything I do, I do heartily as to the Lord and not to men, knowing that I serve Christ. I am receiving the reward of the inheritance He has provided for me. (See Colossians 3:23-24.)

72. My tongue is filled with life, not death, and I will eat of its fruit. My speech is seasoned with grace and salt, and in Christ I am confident how I should answer every person. (See Proverbs 18:21; Colossians 4:6.)

73. The blood of Jesus Christ cleanses me from all filthiness of the flesh and spirit, and perfects holiness in me. (See Second Corinthians 7:1.)

74. Because I am submitted to God, I resist the devil and he flees from me. (See James 4:7.)

75. In Christ, I have been given authority to trample on all the power and works of the devil. *Nothing*, absolutely nothing, will by any means hurt me. (See Luke 10:19.)

76. Because I believe on the Lord Jesus Christ, I am saved and all my household will be saved. (See Acts 16:31.)

77. In Christ I live and move and have my being. (See Acts 17:28.)

78. In all things, I am more than a conqueror through Him who loves me. (See Romans 8:37.)

79. I will pray in another tongue in the Holy Spirit, for therein is the rest and refreshing of the Lord. In this manner, my faith will also be built up. (See Isaiah 28:11-12; Jude 1:20.)

80. In Christ I have been made a king and a priest to God, my Father. (See Revelation 1:6.)

81. I hunger and thirst for righteousness. (See Matthew 5:6.)

82. Because my ways please the Lord, He makes even my enemies to be at peace with me. (See Proverbs 16:7.)

83. The Holy Spirit guides me into all truth and reveals things to me that are to happen in the future. He is my Comforter, Counselor, Helper, Advocate, Intercessor, Strengthener, and Standby. (See John 15:26; 16:13 AMP.)

84. I am far from oppression, for I will not fear. I am far from terror, for it will not come near me. (See Isaiah 54:14.)

85. My children are taught of the Lord and are obedient to His will. Great is their peace and undisturbed composure. (See Isaiah 54:13 AMP.)

86. Because I know the voice of the Good Shepherd, Jesus Christ, I follow Him. I will not follow the voice of a stranger. (See John 10:4-5,27.)

87. I am led by the Spirit of God. I am God's son (or daughter). The law of the Spirit of life in Christ Jesus has set me free from the law of sin and death. (See Romans 8:2,14.)

88. Because I revere and worship the Lord, the Sun of Righteousness has arisen in my life with healing in His wings. I will go forth like a calf released from the stall and leap for joy! (See Malachi 4:2 AMP.)

89. Because I give, it is given unto me, good measure, pressed down, shaken together, and running over. With the same measure I give, it is given back to me. (See Luke 6:38.)

90. Because I am quick to forgive, God is quick to forgive me. With God's help, I will love my enemies, do good to those who hate me, and bless those who curse me and spitefully use me. (See Mark 11:25-26; Luke 6:27-28.)

91. I am blessed because I give to the poor. The Lord will deliver me in times of trouble. He will preserve me and keep me alive, and I will be blessed on the earth. God will not deliver me to the will of my enemies, but He will strengthen and sustain me. Light, healing, and righteousness will come forth speedily in my behalf. The glory of the Lord will be my rear guard. When I call, the Lord will answer, and when I cry, He will say, "Here I am!" (See Psalm 41:1-3; Isaiah 58:6-9.)

92. The salt and light of the Lord Jesus Christ radiate from me, causing the lost to want to know the Source of it. (See Matthew 5:13-16.)

93. By choice, I am a laborer in God's harvest fields. I am a channel of healing for the sick and those with incurable diseases, of resurrection power for the dead and deliverance for the demon oppressed. As I share God's Word, He confirms it with signs, wonders, and miracles. (See Matthew 9:37-38; 10:8; Mark 16:15-20.)

94. Repentance and acceptance of Jesus Christ as my Lord and Savior have wiped away my sins and have caused times of refreshing to come in the presence of the Lord. (See Acts 3:19.)

95. My faith is strong and continually growing from hearing and hearing the Word of God. Like Abraham, I speak those things which do not yet exist as though they already are. (See Romans 10:17; 4:17.)

96. Eye has not seen, nor ear heard, nor has it entered into the heart of man the things God has prepared for me, simply because I love Him! (See First Corinthians 2:9.)

97. I will speak pleasant words, for they are a source of sweetness to the soul and health to the bones: for myself as well as for others. (See Proverbs 16:24.)

98. Create in me a clean heart, O God, and renew a steadfast, right spirit within me. Do not cast me away from your presence, or take Your Holy Spirit from me. (See Psalm 51:10-11.)

99. I have no lack in any area of my life, because God owns the cattle on a thousand hills. (See Psalm 50:10.)

100. The name of the Lord is a tower of strength. I run into it and am safe and secure. (See Proverbs 18:10 Moffatt.)

About the Author

BILLY JOE DAUGHERTY is founder and pastor of Victory Christian Center, a church with membership of over 10,000 in Tulsa, Oklahoma. He is also founder of Victory Christian School, Victory Bible Institute, and Victory World Missions Training Center. Other Victory Bible Institutes have been started over 18 countries worldwide, with several others starting in the next year.

Pastor Daugherty has conducted monthly crusades in Tulsa's low-income housing projects since January 1989, seeing over 6,000 decisions for Christ. He has also preached 24 crusades in Russia, with over 500,000 decisions for Christ made since November 1991.

Pastor Daugherty is a graduate of Oral Roberts University, with a Master's degree, and he has attended Rhema Bible Training Center and Christ for the Nations. He serves as vice-chairman of the Oral Roberts University Board of Regents and is a member of the board of Pentecostal/Charismatic Churches of North America. He is also the Executive Director of International Charismatic Bible Ministries.

Pastor Daugherty and his wife, Sharon, are the parents of four children: Sarah, Ruth, John, and Paul.

Other Books by
Pastor Billy Joe Daugherty

Led by the Spirit
Principles of Prayer
Killing the Giant of Ministry Debt
You Can Be Healed
Building Stronger Marriages and Families
The Demonstration of the Gospel
Living in God's Abundance

To contact Pastor Daugherty, please write or call:

Victory Christian Center
7700 South Lewis
Tulsa, OK 74136-7700
Telephone: 918-491-7700

Additional copies of this book and other
book titles from DESTINY IMAGE are
available at your local bookstore.

Call toll-free: 1-800-722-6774.

Send a request for a catalog to:

Destiny Image₍ᵣ₎ Publishers, Inc.
P.O. Box 310
Shippensburg, PA 17257-0310

"Speaking to the Purposes of God for This
Generation and for the Generations to Come"

**For a complete list of our titles,
visit us at www.destinyimage.com**